INFAMY & AFTERMATH

PEARL HARBOR, THEN AND NOW

By Scott C. S. Stone

Pearl Harbor Then and Now
*explores the **prelude** to the Pearl Harbor attack,*
*the **infamous raid** itself,*
*and the **repercussions** that echoed*
through the next 50 years.

☆ ☆ ☆

Fifty years ago Pearl Harbor awoke to the screaming of engines and the sudden savagery of bombs and bullets... a horror that shattered more than the Sunday morning calm; it shook America out of its complacency and knit the nation into a formidable power.

United as never before, Americans mobilized and fought...and won. Then they helped the former enemy rebuild a broken nation. But the end of the war was not the beginning of peace. The next 50 years were a half-century of repression and brutality and new kinds of war.

For many Americans, history began on that violent Sunday at Pearl Harbor, and all future events were measured against the solemn import of that day. *INFAMY AND AFTERMATH - Pearl Harbor Then and Now* explores the **prelude** to the Pearl Harbor attack, the **infamous raid** itself, and the **repercussions** that echoed through the next 50 years.

Target: Pearl Harbor

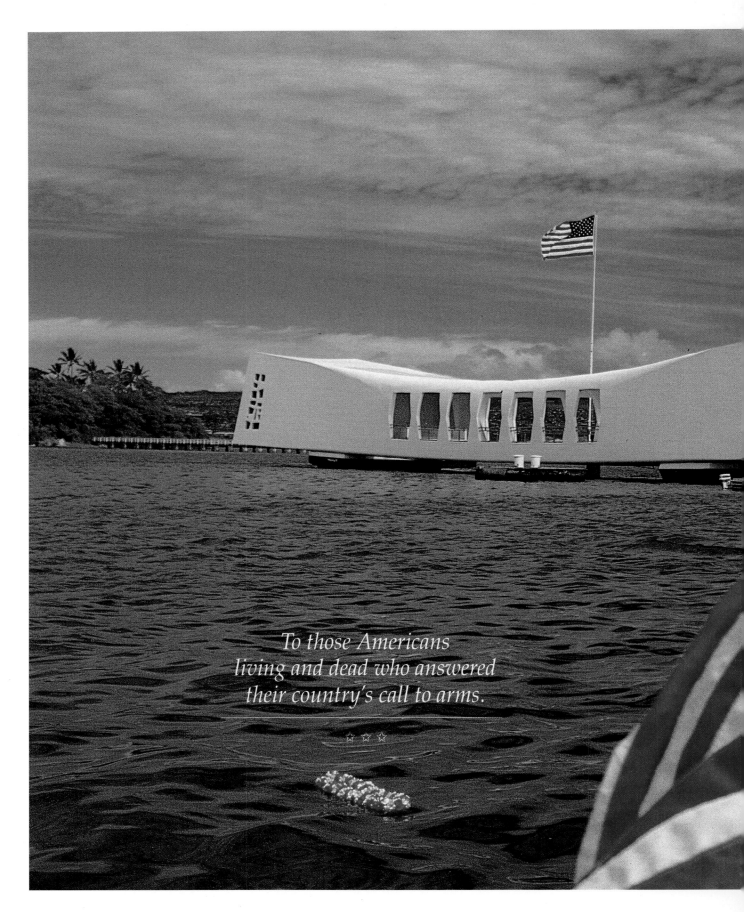

*To those Americans
living and dead who answered
their country's call to arms.*

☆ ☆ ☆

Carl Shaneff

The sound of the bell of Gionshoja
echoes the impermanence of all things.
The hue of the flowers of the teak tree declare
that they who flourish must be brought low.
Yea, the proud ones are but for a moment,
like an evening dream in springtime.
The mighty are destroyed at the last, they
are as the dust before the wind.

HEIKE MONOGATARI
a chronicle of the Samurai

CONTENTS

Despite this spectacular explosion, the USS Shaw survived, was refitted with a new bow, and got back into action within a year.

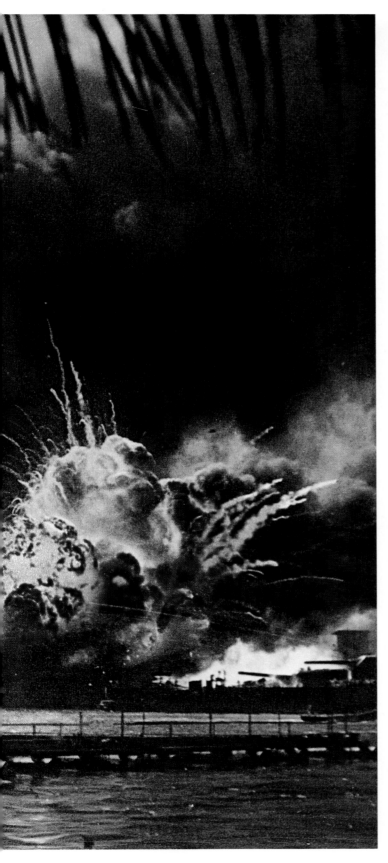

When the trade winds move across the waters of the harbor, the small waves lap against the docks and the pilings and the gray hulls of the ships, and the wind brings the sound of church bells, signalling the Mass. The sunlight splintering on the rim of Diamond Head hurls shafts of light across the surface of the water, and the clouds begin building over the interior of the island, along the peaks of the mountain ranges.

On a Sunday morning a visitor stands at the Merry Point landing and looks across Pearl Harbor. He knows a vague unease, because the calmness of the morning evokes memories of another such morning a half-century ago, and the high drama and sudden deaths of that time resonate in his heart and mind. Across the harbor come faintly the voices of men long dead, and the whine of engines and the monstrous anger of the guns. The sound of church bells now becomes melancholy and fades in the rising din of battle, and in his mind's eye the visitor sees the huge ships shudder and begin to die. The sun is darkened by the roiling smoke rising even higher than the aircraft that spin and dart like angry bees.

The ghostly voices rise in surprise, or supplication or shock. The visitor has a taste in his mouth like copper, and images glide in and out, too swift to hold, too vivid to forget — a blood-covered sailor firing at an onrushing aircraft with the rising sun on its wings, another sailor flaming like a torch as he is pulled from the oil-soaked and blazing waters, yet another dying silently as he topples from the bridge of a battleship to disappear below the dark surface.

On this Sunday morning, time has dulled the images, but not erased them, and the air that a moment before was perfumed with flowers now carries the scent of murder. The visitor squints anxiously toward the north, half expecting another formation of aircraft to break the clouds and split into sections to continue the attack.

The images recede, the sounds become muted. The visitor shakes his head and looks up at a calm morning, and silent skies. To his left is a nest of modern destroyers, and farther down Bravo Pier are a couple of Fast Frigates and a Guided Missile Cruiser, classes of ships carrying equipment unknown fifty years ago. Elsewhere in the harbor are submarines that run on nuclear power, and an aircraft carrier that has little resemblance to the flattops of a half-century earlier.

The visitor is reassured. It is not 1941, and on this Sunday the harbor and the naval base and the ships and

The USS California lists to starboard in the moments following her attack.

aircraft lie peacefully beneath a great, yellow, Hawaiian sun. But even as the visitor turns and walks from the pier the images still echo in his mind, forever a part of him.

For many Americans, history began that Sunday morning and from thereon they would measure events in time by whether they occurred before or after the attack. For the attackers and the defenders, for those who simply were there, it was perhaps the most dramatic moment of their lives and they — and the world — would never be the same. Even after fifty years, they would look back and recall that time as vividly as if it had been yesterday, and measure the other great events of their era against those few hours on a terrible morning in December.

At Pearl Harbor the afternoon of December 7, 1941, was a continuum of horror. Smoke hung in the soft Hawaiian air. Flames flared and died and flared again. The stench of burned flesh and burned timbers lay over the harbor, and it was the same at the other military bases on the island of Oahu. The distant sound of sirens was eclipsed by the shouts of desperate, angry men and the cries of the wounded. When darkness fell, the night was shattered by gunfire from trigger-happy sentries firing at spectres, expecting an invasion by the forces that had that morning brought death and destruction out of a calm sky.

North of the Hawaiian Islands a powerful Japanese task force steamed away from the scene with rejoicing aboard the ships; surprise had been achieved, the attack had gone as planned, and Japanese losses — five midget submarines and 29 aircraft — were remarkably light. Japan regarded Hawaii as a rightful part of an expanding em-

pire, as a "historic" part of Japan's Pacific sovereignty, and the first step had been taken to recover the Islands.

Planning for the next step began the day after the Pearl Harbor raid.

"Eastern Operation" was designed to put Japanese troops ashore in Hawaii and to use the Islands to blockade American forces heading west across the sea. Hawaii could also serve as a staging base for the ultimate landing of the troops on the American West Coast if that became necessary. The most important reason for taking Hawaii, however, was political: The Japanese believed that the seizure of Hawaii would bring America to the negotiating table and forestall a long war.

The invasion of Hawaii very nearly took place. Only a decisive American victory six months later at the Battle of Midway – a defeat that stunned the Japanese and forced a change in their strategy–turned Japan aside from a second bold attack on Hawaii.

Meanwhile, Japan appeared unstoppable. Throughout the Pacific and Asia the Imperial Japanese forces rolled up victory after victory — Manila and Singapore and Hong Kong...Guam, Rabaul and Wake Island.

But it was Pearl Harbor that drew America into war, and within hours of the attack the world was assessing what had happened that Sunday morning. England breathed a sigh of relief, feeling that America's entrance into the war would insure victory. (Winston Churchill's immediate reaction was, "so we had won after all.") American reaction was the swift airing of a collective guilt, a consensus that the nation should have been better prepared, given all the various signs and portents. Mobilization was quick, and President Franklin D. Roosevelt had hardly signed the declaration of war against Japan at 4:10 p.m. on December 8 than America began the long road back from what the President called "the date which will live in infamy."

Japanese military professionals were going through their own agonizing reappraisal. The rationale for the raid was clear enough to the man who planned it, Admiral Isoroku Yamamoto. He feared America's industrial prowess and a war of attrition with the United States. Yamamoto came to regard the attack on the Pacific Fleet as a necessity, and the invasion of Hawaii as a military means of forcing America to negotiate peace.

In a prophetic statement to Japan's Prime Minister Fumimori Konoe, Yamamoto said, "If I am told to fight regardless of consequences, I shall run wild for the first six months or a year, but I have utterly no confidence for the second or third years."

Now Yamamoto and others in the military hierarchy began to take a cold look at the Pearl Harbor attack. While the Japanese citizenry remained euphoric, the military began a descent into gloom.

The attack had failed to catch any U.S. aircraft carriers in port, carriers which would be prowling for revenge. The attack failed to destroy the oil tanks that would fuel the retaliation. It failed to destroy the submarine base. It failed to destroy the repair facilities at Pearl Harbor. Above all else, it aroused the fury of Americans in a way the Japanese had not expected in a society they considered soft and decadent. For if America had been too casual in its assessment of the Japanese character, so had Japan failed to take the measure of the American.

The attack on Pearl Harbor, far from being the Japanese triumph it first appeared, began to assume its true proportions: it was a terrible blunder.

☆ ☆ ☆

CHAPTER ONE

PRELUDE TO WAR

National Archives

Japanese envoys Admiral Nomura and Saburo Kurusu leave the U.S. State Department near the time the Japanese task force was striking Pearl Harbor. Files revealed the envoys often were denied information from their own government about the pending attack on Oahu.

At the turn of the century, there were nuances in Japanese lives that few, if any, Americans recognized. There was an expansion of Japanese thought, a new curiosity about the world, and a determination that Japan have a place in it. The attitude of an emerging Japan toward the United States was a topic of endless exploration in the early part of the 1900s, but again, few could tell precisely what that attitude was.

Since Commodore Matthew Perry "opened" Japan to the modern world in 1853-54, America and Japan had been trading partners and friends. Yet there was an accumulation of tension as well. The militarists in Japan began to rise to power (with a concomitant rise in suspicions by some Americans) and in 1937 troops invaded China as the first step in a pattern of conquest. Two years later Japan occupied Hainan Island, off the southern coast of China, and shortly afterwards laid claim to the Spratlys, strategic coral islands in the South China Sea.

For many in the West it was simply a confirmation of Japanese militarism at its most extreme; others hoped it was possible to curb the Japanese excesses, and perhaps even arrange a withdrawal of Japanese forces from China. But in 1940, France fell and Japanese forces moved into French Indo–china. In September of that year the die was cast when Japan signed the Tripartite Pact with Germany and Italy, putting Japan squarely in the Axis camp.

Japan again looked south, this time toward Malaya, the Philippines, and the Dutch East Indies. By the time 1941 dawned there were people on both sides of the vast Pacific Ocean who began to feel that war between Japan and the United States was inevitable.

One of them was Joseph Grew, the U.S. Ambassador to Japan, who held a genuine fondness for Japan but was not given to illusions. He picked up a strong rumor that Japan would launch a surprise attack against the U.S. Pacific Fleet, and passed the rumor along. Washington Intelligence circles discounted the report. Grew also wrote President Franklin D. Roosevelt a personal letter, stating his belief that a showdown was coming.

By the end of 1940 an uneasy U.S. government had cut Japan off from all vital war material except total oil supplies – in July of that year taking control of exports of aviation fuel and scrap iron and steel. A partial but damaging embargo on oil was imposed in mid-summer, and it had the immediate effect of enraging the Japanese.

The Japanese now began to identify a strong need to keep America immobilized in the Pacific in order to allow Japanese expansion into other areas of Asia and the Pacific. For those in Tokyo still hoping for peace, the Japanese ambassador sent to the United States was a reason for optimism. Kichisaburo Nomura was a 64-year-old former admiral who felt at home in the U.S. Well-liked and respected, Nomura had a number of American friends including President Roosevelt. But what was expected of Nomura was more than anyone could have accomplished, given the determination of Japanese militarists. He was no sooner at sea than Japanese leaders resumed talking bombastically about the "Greater East Asia Co-Prosperity Sphere "– a nebulous area that could be, and mean, whatever the Japanese wanted. There were few doubts about Japanese plans to rule Asia, and to force out the hated West-

In 1924 the Japanese cruiser Asano sails past Oahu's Koko Head.

erners – the Americans, British, French and Dutch – who were viewed as colonialists and whose sun in Asia was setting.

If diplomacy would not sway the Americans, war was inevitable.

Against this backdrop, a most unlikely war planner began to think about an attack on the Americans at Pearl Harbor. Admiral Isoroku Yamamoto was an ardent loyalist, loyal to the Emperor and to Japan. But he was a hard-eyed realist as well. When he thought about Japan taking on the Americans and their allies, he began to see a war of attrition that Japan could not win: Japan was still fighting a war with China, and was committed on several other fronts as well. When his thoughts settled on what he felt was a workable solution, Yamamoto wrote a letter in his capacity as Commander of the Combined Fleet to a fellow admiral, in which he said Japan's real hope was to destroy the U.S. Pacific Fleet at the outset

of the war. This, he hoped, would sap the desire of the American people to get involved in what could be a long war. A tough, smart and experienced military professional, Yamamoto believed he had hit upon the solution to keeping America out of a prolonged war. But in reality, his plan led to the act that united Americans as never before.

In the summer of 1939 Americans had their own realities to face: war seemed inevitable and the nation was not prepared. But the strategists saw the danger as coming from the Axis powers, and a joint military board strongly advised that the U.S. Navy be defensive, merely holding Hawaii – and probably abandoning the Philippines. In the end, President Roosevelt approved a plan that included the defense of Hawaii, Wake Island and Samoa, but which left Guam and the Philippines to their fate. Meanwhile, America was engaged in a cautious policy

This mock-up of Ford Island and Battleship Row in Pearl Harbor was made for a propaganda film in Japan after the attack.

of assisting, in minor ways, British efforts against the Nazis in violation of neutrality laws; President Roosevelt personally stretched those laws by offering some assistance, spurred on in part by a report from a group of physicists, including Albert Einstein, that the Germans were working on an atomic bomb. These developments, along with continued Nazi successes as war raged across Europe, drew the attention of America across the Atlantic.

Yamamoto continued with the plan to attack Pearl Harbor, now called Operation Z. The Japanese faced technical problems, such as developing torpedoes that would

run in the relatively shallow waters of Pearl Harbor, and adapting heavy Naval artillery shells into bombs that would penetrate the steel decks of aircraft carriers and other major ships. Yamamoto assembled some of the best creative and technical minds in Japan – among them Commander Minoru Genda, Vice Admiral Shigeru Fukudome, Commander Kosei Maeda, Rear Admiral Takijiro Onishi, and the man who would actually lead the Pearl Harbor attack, Commander Mitsuo Fuchida.

Practice sessions began in Kagoshima, in southern Kyushu. Area residents became accus-

tomed to aircraft screaming a few feet above the tops of buildings as they angled themselves for dummy torpedo runs across Kagoshima Bay. As the relationship between Japan and the United States continued to deteriorate, the Japanese planners came to feel the raid actually would take place, and went about their preparations with a grim intensity.

In spite of the worsening situation, both Washington and Hawaii shared an air of complacency, which seemed to fly in the face of all logic. In August 1940 American cryptographers had broken the Japanese diplomatic codes, including one designated Purple, a most

Admiral Isoroku Yamamoto predicted success in the surprise attack on Pearl Harbor.

The code machine that broke the Purple code and provided Allied forces with an astonishing amount of information.

secret code the Japanese felt could not be broken. From August on the messages that passed between Tokyo and its embassies abroad were being read by Americans as well. At times the U.S. knew more about Tokyo's intentions than Admiral Nomura – and it often appeared that Tokyo was not rushing to tell Nomura all that was going on in the homeland. Breaking the Purple code and others fell under its own code word, Magic. Despite the obvious benefits provided by the code-breakers, however, they had failed to crack the naval codes, which meant the U.S. never picked up Yamamoto's messages to the Japanese task force that ultimately sailed from the Kurile Islands to attack Pearl Harbor. Additionally, Pearl Harbor never received any of the Purple cipher machines, although the U.S. sent three of them to London.

☆ ☆ ☆

A reluctant military leader, Emperor Hirohito shunned wartime demands.

CHAPTER TWO

National Archives

Enjoying the calm before the storm, Pearl Harbor prior to 1941 was not considered by U.S. leaders to be the primary target of a Japanese raid.

THE WAR CLOUDS GATHER

In Hawaii at any one time might be six or eight battleships, one or two aircraft carriers and any number of smaller vessels. Army troops at Schofield Barracks and Fort Shafter numbered close to 25,000 men, and around the shorelines were 127 fixed coastal defense guns. There were confident predictions that no enemy attacker could get close to the islands without being seen, and that pursuit planes from Oahu airbases would engage any enemy up to 750 miles away (this latter assertion was startling, given the fact that there were no aircraft on Oahu that could fly 750 miles out and still engage an enemy in battle). Oahu's defend-

ers talked confidently of having on hand 35 B-17s, 35 medium-range bombers, 13 light bombers, and 150 pursuit planes. However, when the raid actually commenced there were 12 B-17s available, not 35, and only six of the 12 could fly.

Also on Oahu were approximately 160,000 members of the Japanese community. About 40,000 were *issei*, first-generation immigrants who were denied U.S. citizenship and had every reason to be proud of Japan's rise to power – they were still Japanese citizens, after all, and their loyalty properly belonged to the Emperor and the land of their birth. Their children were *Nisei*, second-generation, for

whom the war would bring poignant and divisive feelings; they were both American and Japanese, and they had to choose which country to fight for. A small minority went off to fight for Japan. Their reasons for doing so included the denial of citizenship to their parents, racial incidents that may have occurred in Hawaii, and what some felt were a lack of opportunities to advance financially and socially in America. *Nisei* who held dual citizenship had to apply to the Japanese government for deferment from the draft, and some who failed to do so actually were drafted and served in the Japanese armed forces. *Nisei* also made up the 100th Battalion, U.S. Army, and coupled with the predominantly *nisei* 442nd Regimental Combat Team, went on to compile one of the most distinguished combat records of any American fighting unit.

(Despite the large Japanese community, and despite warnings that sabotage would occur if war began, there were no incidents of sabotage in Hawaii. The only spying efforts came from the Japanese consulate, where a bogus consular official who was really a naval Ensign kept tabs on the ships coming and going in Pearl Harbor, and relayed that information to Tokyo.)

Heading the military forces in Hawaii were the Pacific Fleet Commander in Chief, Admiral Husband E. Kimmel, and the Army's Hawaiian Department commander, Lieutenant General Walter C. Short. Both men took over their commands within a few days of each other early in 1941. On November 27, 1941, both received an alert based on *Magic*'s monitoring of the Japanese message traffic. The alert said that negotiations with Japan apparently were terminated, and that future actions of the Japanese were unpredictable but probably hostile at any moment. It added that if hostilities were unavoidable it was desired that Japan should commit the first hostile act.

General Short received the message with an addendum that he act without alarming the civilian population in Hawaii, and he thus interpreted the whole message as a warning against sabotage. Admiral Kimmel received the alert, with a stronger note attached, calling the message a warning. But also included was an Intelligence summary that the Japanese were expected to strike in Borneo, the Philippines, or along Thailand's Kra Isthmus. Thus both Kimmel and Short received warnings that some act of aggression was likely, but where and when remained obscure.

Three days after these messages were received a Japanese strike force consisting of six aircraft carriers sailing in three columns and flanked by escorting battleships and cruisers, refueled in the North Pacific from accompanying tankers. They were halfway from Tankan Bay, in the Kuriles, to their targets in Hawaii. More than 200 miles ahead of them, Japanese submarines were on the lookout for any vessels.

On December 1, Japan's Prime Minister Hideki Tojo told an Imperial conference that included the Emperor, "Matters have reached the point where Japan must begin war with the United States, Great Britain, and the Netherlands to preserve her Empire." Code signals went out to ships to be ready for an offensive against the Philippines and Malaya, and the Pearl Harbor strike force was unleashed with the words, *Niitaka Yama Nobore* – climb Mount Niitaka.

On December 5, the carrier *USS Lexington* put to sea from Pearl Harbor to ferry Marine Corps aircraft to Midway. That same day in Washington, the Japanese diplomatic mission was summoned to the State Department to explain why large Japanese convoys were moving across the South China Sea. America's top leadership became convinced that the impending Japanese action, which by now all were expecting, would be directed toward Thailand.

On December 6 in Singapore, the British decided to move advance troops to the Thai border but not to cross it and give the Japanese an excuse to attack. In Washington, President Roosevelt sent a personal telegram to the Emperor Hirohito asking him, in the name of humanity, to prevent the death and destruction that would result from a Japanese attack on Thailand. Soon after, the President received the bad news that Japan had rejected his earlier 10-point proposal for peaceful solutions to the deteriorating situation.

On the afternoon of December 6, the Japanese task force was 600 miles north of Hawaii, and Admiral Yamamoto's message was broadcast to all hands: "The rise or fall of the Empire depends upon the battle. Everyone will do his duty with utmost efforts."

On the night of December 6, the servicemen of Oahu generally were unconcerned about the war alert; there had been so many that they were routine. Along Battleship Row at Ford Island the dreadnoughts were lying peacefully in the soft night. In Honolulu the soldiers and sailors were in the bars or theaters, and at Hickam Field, Wheeler, Schofield Barracks, the Naval Air Station at Kaneohe, and the Marine Corps Air Station at Ewa, bored guards were patroling the perimeters, their thoughts elsewhere. Civilians were going about their own affairs, and as dusk settled over Hawaii it was just another beautiful evening in one of the world's most peaceful places.

CHAPTER THREE

TO...TO...TO

National Archives

It was the darkest part of the night when the U.S. mine-sweeper *Condor* sighted a periscope off the entrance to Pearl Harbor about 3:45 a.m. and promptly notified the destroyer *USS Ward*, the guard vessel patrolling off the harbor entrance. The Ward steamed over and conducted a fruitless two-hour search.

Three hours later three PBY flying boats armed with depth charges flew routine scouting missions off Oahu's southern coast. Below them, the *Ward* continued to prowl the harbor area and suddenly, at 6:37 a.m. found a small submarine trailing the supply ship *Antares*, as she slipped past the harbor boom and entered Pearl Harbor. The *Ward* went to full speed and opened fire. The destroyer's second salvo blew open the submarine's "sail" (conning tower) and set the submarine up for the depth charge attack that followed. A few minutes later the Ward signalled Naval Control Center, "We have attacked, fired upon and dropped depth charges upon sub operating in defensive area." The message took almost an hour to reach Admiral Kimmel, who asked for an amplification of the message. No one knew it at the time, but the *Ward* had fired the first shots for America at Pearl Harbor.

Dive bombers warm up on the deck of a Japanese carrier in preparation for the Pearl Harbor attack.

Pearl Harbor as seen through the eyes of the attackers. This photo also shows smoke rising over Hickam Field in the distance, one of many targets.

Admiral Chuichi Nagumo commanded the task force that hammered Pearl Harbor.

A half-hour later, one of the PBYs depth-charged another submarine contact. The pilot sent his report in code, which took more than a half hour to get cleared and circulated. At approximately the same time, two radar operators at Kahuku Point, in the northernmost part of Oahu, reported a huge flight of aircraft approaching the Island. A duty officer believed them to be a flight of B-17s expected to arrive that day from the West Coast. "Don't worry about it," the radar operators were told.

Out at sea, two reconnaissance aircraft launched at 5 a.m. by the Japanese task force flew undetec-ted in a sky of partial clouds under a bright yellow sun. The weather reports promised a warm and sunny day. At 6 a.m., the Imperial Navy battle ensign was broken out on the masthead of the aircraft *Akagi* , and the admiral in charge of the strike force, Vice Admiral Chuichi Nagumo, looked with satisfaction on his powerful armada. In addition to the *Akagi* were the carriers *Kaga*, *Soryu*, *Hiryu*, *Zuikaku* and *Shokaku*, accompanied by the battleships *Heie* and *Kirishima* and various cruisers, destroyers and support ships. Thirty-one ships in total, they had sailed undetected across the North Pacific, taking advantage of fog and inclement weather that, ironically, had caused other ships to take the southern route across the Pacific. They were 220 miles north of

Oahu, and the die was cast.

Commander Mitsuo Fuchida fastened the *hachimaki* headband given him by the *Akagi*'s crew and led his flight of aircraft aloft into the blue Hawaiian sky. The first wave of attacking planes totaled 183 – 49 bombers with armor piercing shells, 40 "Kate" torpedo bombers, 51 dive bombers and, flying escort above them, 43 Zeros. It was the fastest launch time the carriers had ever managed, and only two aircraft failed to make it off the decks.

An hour and forty minutes later Fuchida's aircraft were deploying over the northern coastline of Oahu, the first wave of the 350 aircraft to be thrown against the Pacific Fleet, still lying passively in Pearl Harbor. Meanwhile, Nagumo turned the First Air Fleet south, then east into the wind and launched the second wave. He then turned the armada south again, taking up a position 180 miles north of Oahu.

Fuchida's pilot now was homing in on a local radio station – the same one which was guiding the unsuspecting B-17s in from the West Coast. At 7:49 a.m. Fuchida ordered his pilot to tap out the signal to attack, the first syllable of *totsugekiseyo* – charge! The pilot sent the signal to all pilots, "To...To...To...."

The dive bombers climbed to 15,000 feet and split into two graceful, deadly, arcing groups. One minute after the attack signal the torpedo bombers divided and banked into position, one flight screaming for the west side of Pearl Harbor, the other swinging north and west and aimed directly at Battleship Row.

Wallowing ignominiously in the surf, a Japanese two-man submarine lies useless on the beach at Bellows Field, Windward Oahu, after the attack.

Moments later came the second signal from Fuchida, the signal that the Fleet had been desperately hoping to hear: it was the Japanese word for tiger – "Tora...tora...tora!" It meant they had achieved complete surprise.

In the center of the harbor alongside Ford Island lay the great gray ships, somnolent and sun-drenched in the calm morning hours. The battleship *California* was moored alone. The battleships *USS Maryland* and *USS Oklahoma* were side by side, with the *Maryland* inboard. The battleships *USS Tennessee* and *USS West Virginia* also were paired, with the *Tennessee* inboard to Ford Island. The *USS Arizona* was inboard of the repair ship *USS Vestal*, and directly behind the *Arizona* was the battleship *USS Nevada*. The eighth battleship, the *USS Pennsylvania,* was resting easily in Drydock One at the Navy Yard across from Ford Island.

In the repair basin were two 10,000-ton cruisers, the *USS New Orleans* and the *USS San Francisco*. Also in harbor were four other 10,000 ton cruisers; the *USS Phoenix* was moored north of Ford Island and the *USS St. Louis, USS Helena*, and *USS Honolulu* were in docks at the Navy yard. Northwest of Ford Island were the 7,000-ton cruisers *USS Raleigh* and *USS Detroit*. To the north and west of the Island were 29 destroyers, 26 of them built after 1933 and thus considered new vessels. In various other slots around the harbor were five submarines, a gunboat, 11 minesweepers, 23 auxiliary ships, nine minelayers and a scattering of smaller craft – altogether more than 130 vessels.

On the *Oklahoma* the watch had been piped to breakfast and on several other ships the gun crews were being relieved and were wiping dew from the anti-aircraft batteries. A small boat put out from the Merry Point landing. Sailors from Ford Island stood idly, watching the sun scattering diamonds of light on the calm harbor waters.

On the *Tennessee* a mess cook stood on deck, sipping coffee and enjoying a morning of typical loveliness. Across the water came the sound of church bells, gently signaling the 8 a.m. Mass.

In the air above, Fuchida had fired a single flare to get the aircraft in proper attack formation. Noticing that one of his flight leaders failed to see it, he fired a second one which was promptly misinterpreted: it sent the dive bombers into action ahead of the slower torpedo-bombers.

The dive bombers swarmed over Ford Island in a burst of fury, loosing bombs on aircraft and hangars below. Moments later the torpedo-bombers skimmed over the harbor's surface, their torpedoes fitted with wooden fins for shallow running. Now the harbor rocked with explosions and the smoke began to billow.

The control tower at Ford Island broadcast an alarm: "Air raid, Pearl Harbor. This is not a drill." Admiral Kimmel's headquarters relayed the signal to outlying Pacific Fleet commands, and it was soon received in Washington.

The *Oklahoma* took three torpedoes and began to list. The *Arizona* heaved ponderously when a bomb exploded in her forward powder magazine, and an intense fire broke out in the heart of the ship, partially obscuring her superstructure.

Sailors watch as aircraft are destroyed on Ford Island.

The date that will live in infamy saw the smashing of the USS Downes and USS Cassin, but the USS Pennsylvania (background) suffered only minor damages and was ready for action two weeks later.

The *West Virginia* took torpedoes, then two heavy bombs, which ignited a fire amidships. Another torpedo passed underneath the minelayer *USS Oglala* and slammed into the *Helena* before exploding. A bomb fell between the two ships, also exploding.

Two torpedoes hammered the *USS Utah*, formerly a battleship and now an American target and gunnery training vessel. The *Utah* began to list to port and sailors jumped from her deck into the water, only to be strafed by passing Japanese planes.

Two more torpedoes struck the *Oklahoma* even as she was capsizing, and men ran desperately along the canted hull. In drydock, the Pennsylvania was jolted by a bomb blast.

The *Tennessee*, moored inboard, escaped the torpedoes, but took two bombs that threw debris about her decks. The *West Virginia* also took two bombs and buckled under their force, then the stricken ship was hit with six torpedoes and began to settle in the water, her main deck awash.

The *Arizona* was hit again. The armor-piercing bomb that had exploded in her magazine also dropped two gun turrets and the ship's conning tower 20 feet below their positions. A number of aerial bombs struck the dying ship, throwing vast amounts of oil into the water around her, which burned for two and a half days.

The *Nevada* managed to get underway, the only ship of her class to do so that terrible morning. Hit in the forward section by a torpedo, she lurched into the channel waters and made for the open sea. At the southwestern point of Ford Island she was rocked by bombs that smashed huge holes into her deck and set her superstructure aflame. As she raced for the chan-

nel entrance, 14th Naval District headquarters had to make a choice – run her aground, or risk her sinking in the channel and blocking it. The *Nevada* was ordered to ground herself; she immediately turned shoreward and ran her proud hull onto a point of land near the channel entrance.

Alongside the dying *Arizona*, the repair ship *Vestal* managed to extract herself and move away from the flaming battleship, anchoring again northeast of Ford Island. The *Neosho*, filled with high-octane aviation gas, managed to clear herself as well and escape from the flames. Presumably out of danger, the *Oglala* was moved by tugs but suddenly capsized. Low-flying bombers streaked in and attacked the *Maryland* and then the cruisers and destroyers.

One destroyer, the *USS Monaghan*, had gotten underway and also was speeding for the harbor entrance when from the bridge crew members saw a signal from the *USS Curtiss*: submarine! The *Curtiss* and the *USS Tangier* opened fire on the sub with the *Curtiss* scoring several direct hits. The *Monaghan's* action was direct and effective – it ran right over the submarine, drawing it under her bows and pushing the submarine astern. As it passed, the *Monaghan* dropped depth charges which lifted the destroyer's stern right out of the water, but silenced the submarine forever. The *Monaghan's* momentum carried her into a blazing barge.

The *California* was burning furiously, as oil from the *Arizona* spread around the *California's* stern. Small boats converged on the stricken ships but a taut formation of aircraft screamed in,

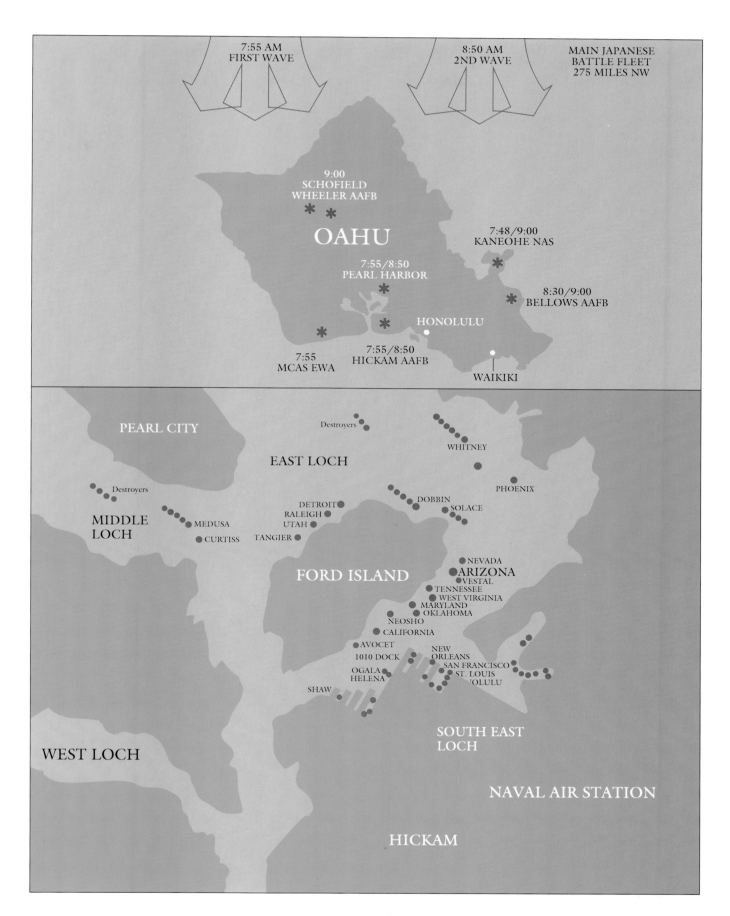

guns blazing, and the bullets smashed into men and boats. In the drydocks the destroyers *USS Cassin* and *USS Downes* flared like giant candles, but the most spectacular blast took place as the destroyer *USS Shaw* took a bomb in her powder magazine that blew away the ship's bow. At the Ford Island Naval Station, a hangar burst into flames and sent long tendrils of smoke skyward.

One of the day's miracles took place on the *USS Raleigh*, where an armor-piercing bomb went all the way through the ship and exploded in the mud of the harbor floor. A torpedo tore into the ship's side, but none of the crew was killed and only a few wounded.

A half-hour after the attack began there was a sudden lull, just as the twelve B-17s flew in on their last gallons of fuel. They came under attack by both sides, landing at various airfields peppered with bullet holes; one smashed into a golf course, and another came apart at the end of the runway at Hickam Field.

The high-altitude bombing resumed when 86 dive-bombers, 54 bombers, and 36 fighters roared around Oahu's east coast. A handful of Army pilots managed to get into the air from Wheeler Field, and shot down 11 Japanese airplanes in dogfights that took place in a sky growing increasingly pock-marked with bursting anti-aircraft shells, and streaked with the smoke from burning ships.

At Wheeler and Ewa, at Hickam Field and Ford Island and Kaneohe, the shattered aircraft blazed furiously. Many of them had been pushed close together on the runways with the idea it would be

easier to guard them against sabotage. This was a clear indication that the military regarded the threat from within greater than the threat from without, and they paid for it as flames leapt from airplane to airplane. Across the field lay the stench of death, in horrible commonality with the scent of murder that came from Pearl Harbor. Bodies lay on runways and taxiways, or charred in the oil-soaked waters of the lochs. The waters that had echoed the soft sounds of the church bells not long before now knew the stuttering of guns, the crump of explo-

sives and the death throes of the great ships.

South of the Islands the aircraft carrier *USS Enterprise* had decided to send 19 aircraft up to Hawaii; they flew innocently into the raid and had no choice except to attempt to land. Six of them went down, four to Japanese fighters, two to American fire.

At Bellows Field on the windward side of Oahu, a midget submarine ran aground and the lone survivor struggled ashore. Captured within minutes, he became the first Japanese prisoner of war to fall to the Americans. Two other

The #2 turrett of the USS Arizona heaves ponderously as the ship decends to its watery grave.

ships had sunk at Pearl Harbor, he refused to believe it – when the attack began he ran out of his quarters, his face pale, the anguish showing in his eyes. Later, as he was standing by his window, a spent bullet broke the glass and left a dark stain on his uniform, but did not injure him. The Admiral murmured, "It would have been merciful if it had killed me."

The *Arizona* died with 1177 men.

The *Oklahoma* sank like some great wounded beast, going down at the stern.

The *West Virginia* settled on the bottom, her deck still awash.

The *Nevada* was rammed onto a point of land, smouldering. The *Utah* capsized.

The *Pennsylvania, Maryland* and *Tennessee* lay hunched and stricken, their wounds severe.

In Honolulu a radio announcer shouted into his microphone, "This is the real McCoy!" A shell detonated near the Governor's home on Beretania Street and the explosion sent shrapnel through the surrounding foliage, killing a pedestrian across the street. Japanese planes strafed the roads leading to the military bases. Four civilians were killed in one car as they hurried toward Pearl Harbor to help rescue workers. About the same time several people were killed when a lunch stand was hit at the corner of Nuuanu and Kukui Streets. Dozens of people fled into the streets when fires engulfed several buildings at King and McCully Streets. Another fire blazed from a large gas tank in the Iwilei area.

At Hickam Field three civilian firemen were killed and seven injured while fighting a spreading blaze. A shell crashed through the roof of a house in Wahiawa, and a nearby hospital took four quick hits. Canefields were blazing in the areas around the bases and sugar plantation firemen ran from fire to fire.

Then, just two hours later in the skies over Oahu, there was only a single aircraft.

It was Fuchida.

He was assessing the devastation below, hardly believing his eyes even as the scene was burned into his mind.

Finally he winged away, unpursued, and landed on the deck of the *Akagi*. He reported to Nagumo and recommended another attack immediately. Nagumo demurred; he was worried about the American carriers which had not been in port. Where were they? Meanwhile, he had radioed back a damage assessment, then imposed a radio silence. Nagumo was still enjoying the feeling that his task force had gotten away with a colossal victory, and he had no intention of taking additional risks. Saying that "anticipated results have been achieved" he ran up a signal on *Akagi's* masthead. It was the order to turn and speed away.

Fuchida had good reason for recommending another attack on Pearl Harbor. While the Japanese plan had been to decimate the Pacific Fleet, and while it more or less ignored other possible targets, Fuchida realized that these targets were there for the taking. His instinct and training told him they would be important to America

submarines had been sunk by the *Ward* and the *Monaghan* and two were lost at sea. The failure of the five to do any significant damage haunted the Japanese submarine service all through the war.

At Ewa, nine of the 11 Wildcat fighters were knocked out. At Wheeler, 30 of the new P-40 aircraft were destroyed. At Fort Kamehameha near Hickam Field, American machine gunners knocked down a Zero.

Meanwhile, Admiral Kimmel had ordered full battle alert against the possibility of an invasion. But when told that at least two battle-

Far from any military target, three civilians in this car were killed by shrapnel in the Japanese attack on Pearl Harbor and other Oahu installations.

and starting to focus on air power, with the carriers as the core of the task forces. It would be Navy aircraft that would inflict the first important Japanese defeat. The attack also served to unite Americans in a way that may never have happened before, or since, and the moral outrage of the average U.S. fighting man was a part of his armament.

Of the ships in harbor on that December 7, 18 were sunk or heavily damaged; but they were not written off. The *Arizona* was a total loss, and is today a war memorial. The *Oklahoma* was also a total loss. It was raised to clear the channel but sank again off Oahu as it was being towed away for scrap.

The *California* was raised and repaired and took part in Pacific campaigns. Similarly, the *West Virginia* and *Tennessee* were repaired and saw action throughout the war. The *Nevada*, at the time of the attack the oldest battleship in the fleet, was modernized and

in the war that had now begun.

The potential targets were the repair facilities, the oil tanks and the submarine base. The fact that America could use them quickly was of utmost importance in the months to come.

None of the three aircraft carriers normally found in and around Pearl Harbor were there at the time of the attack, and thus escaped to take a deadly vengeance. The *USS Saratoga* was being repaired on the West Coast, the *USS Enterprise* was returning from Wake Island, and the *USS Lexington* was returning home after ferrying aircraft to Midway. The ninth battleship of the Pacific Fleet, the *USS Colorado*, also escaped, being in the Navy Yard at Bremerton, Washington.

Because the oil tanks and the repair facilities were intact, American submarines and aircraft carriers soon could take the offensive – in a limited way perhaps, but the

offensive all the same.

The Americans also reaped psychological benefits. The devastation created by the attacking Japanese caused America to re-think its naval strategies and techniques, pulling back from the concept of battleships as the heart of the fleet

The Japanese did not escape unscathed from the Pearl Harbor attack, but their losses were relatively light. More damaging was their failure to destroy the Shipyard, the fuel tanks and submarine pens.

used throughout the war. The *Utah* was a total loss. Repaired and put back into service were the battleships *Pennsylvania* and *Maryland*, the cruisers *Helena*, *Honolulu* and *Raleigh*, the minelayer *Oglala*, the destroyers *Shaw*, *Cassin* and *Downes*, the repair ship *Vestal*, and the seaplane tender *Curtiss*. All in all, it was a remarkable record of salvage and repair, an American "can do" effort that was symbolic of the attitudes of the day.

Ninety-two Navy aircraft were destroyed and 31 damaged. The Army Air Corps lost 96 planes and had 128 damaged.

Navy losses were 2001 officers and men killed, 710 wounded. The Army had 240 killed and 364 wounded. The Marines lost 102 and had 69 wounded.

Civilian casualties were 58 killed and 35 wounded. At the end of that terrible raid, total casualties were 2,404 dead and 1,178 wounded.

The Japanese lost 29 aircraft, five midget submarines, and a larger, I-class submarine, and had one man captured.

There was carnage that bloody Sunday. Afterwards, however, in a sober assessment, it started to appear as if the Japanese triumph was an incomplete victory. In time it began to look even worse. Admiral Yamamoto's plans (and he was given to complicated battle strategies) along with those of his colleagues, had not focused on targets that would prove as important as the ships themselves, and the raid began to take on the taint of a large-scale military mistake.

The destruction at Hickam Field included not only hangars and other buildings, but aircraft such as this shattered B-17.

CHAPTER FOUR

DUST BEFORE THE WIND

National Archives

Navy fighters during the attack on the Japanese fleet off Midway, June 4th to 6th 1942. In the center a burning Japanese ship.

Shortly after the attack on Pearl Harbor, Japanese bombers took off from Saipan and went flashing over Guam, where fewer than 500 sailors and Marines armed only with pistols and machine guns faced the prospect of defending an island 30 miles long. The attackers destroyed the Marine barracks and sank the *USS Penguin* in Apra Harbor. Four destroyers had sailed from Japan to be a part of the attacking force, and distant air cover was provided by four of the carriers that had taken part in the Pearl Harbor raid.

On December 10, 700 men of the Japanese Navy's Special Landing Forces stormed ashore at 4 a.m. at Dungas Beach and raced into Agana, Guam's capital. South of the harbor, at Agat, units of the South Seas Detachment, reinforced by elements of the 55th Division, also came ashore.

Eighty Chamorros of the Insular Guard and 28 Marines took on the invaders in a brief but bloody skirmish. But the Navy governor of the island, Captain McMillin, knew the situation was hopeless. Two hours after the invasion he signaled the island's surrender. It was accepted by Major General Tomitaro Horii, in charge of the invasion, and Guam dropped into Japanese hands. The surrender was the beginning of the harsh oppression in which Guamanians were beaten and starved. The situation was to grow worse as American forces approached and the people of Guam were turned into slave labor, forced to dig bunkers and pillboxes as the Japanese, in turn, prepared to defend against invasion.

Wake Island was attacked on December 8 by 36 Japanese bombers. With less than 30 seconds warning and without radar, the garrison watched helplessly as the

30

Jubilant Japanese troops on Bataan, the Philippines, in 1942.

bombers destroyed seven of the Marine Corps fighters just delivered by the Enterprise. A Japanese task force loomed offshore and got into an exchange of gunfire in which two Japanese destroyers were sunk. These were the opening rounds in what was to be a heroic but futile defense of the island. The Japanese withdrew but came back in overwhelming force and finally took the island on the evening of December 23.

The juggernaut rolled on.

The Japanese attacked Hong Kong, where the British fought a delaying action. Japanese air raids struck the Philippines at Baguio, Tuguegarao, and Clark Field. Japanese raiders fell on Thailand. On January 23, 1942, the Japanese took Rabaul, where air cover for the attackers was provided by four of the six carriers that had launched aircraft against Pearl Harbor.

Rabaul fell quickly, followed by the magnificent harbor of Kavieng on New Ireland. These successes fired the Japanese military with tremendous confidence and had an even stronger effect on Japanese civilians. In the euphoria of the moment, there was a general call for ousting all Westerners from Asia entirely – an Asia for the Asians.

But the tide was to turn more swiftly than Japanese planners could have envisioned. And it turned to a great extent because Americans and American aircraft carriers from Hawaii, using fuel that was untouched in the December 7 raid, began to take the war to the Japanese. Not until much later did the second major Japanese mistake involving Hawaii come

back to haunt the war planners – Japan should have invaded Hawaii, and occupied it in the wake of the Pearl Harbor raid. By the time they realized it, it was too late.

More than a decade before the Pearl Harbor raid, Admiral Yamamoto had advocated seizing the Islands in the event of war, and for good reasons. Hawaii was an unsinkable aircraft carrier in the mid-Pacific from which strikes could be made at Japanese forces. It was a staging base for any type of ships. It was a supply and logistics center, a mammoth repair facility, a fortress that must be taken prior to any major attacks against the U.S. West Coast. Perhaps the most brilliant of the attack planners, Commander Minoru Genda, wanted an invasion to follow the surprise attack.

As often happens, inter-service rivalry got in the way of logic. The Japanese Army opposed an invasion of Hawaii because it regarded its commitments in Southeast Asia

An observer who found a Japanese machine gun nest plots in on a map to relay the information back to artillery for a subsequent attack.

as more important, and because its troops might be needed against the Russians. Even within the Navy there was opposition to a Hawaii invasion because the planners wanted a total concentration on South Asia.

Yamamoto had won his argument that the Pacific Fleet had to be immobilized to prevent it from interfering with operations in Southeast Asia; he had threatened to resign if the Pearl Harbor attack was not ordered. He backed away from his invasion concept in the end because he concluded Japan was attempting to do too much with too little.

It was a decision the Admiral regretted in the hours following the attack on Pearl Harbor. After the initial reports of how easily the attack had been accomplished, he ordered planning to begin at once for an invasion and occupation of Hawaii. The plan was called "Eastern Operation," and while it continued to run into opposition from the Army and from elements within the Navy, it began to evolve. In more or less final form it called for an invasion of Hawaii in late 1942 or early 1943, with the resistance in the Islands to be snuffed out by three formidable task forces. The assault would begin on the "Big Island" of Hawaii, then shift to Oahu, whose surrender would bring about the capitulation of the other Islands.

But meanwhile there were the American carriers to be dealt with, and a solution to both situations began to appear – the strategy became to lure the American carriers into a battle they could not win, and to position Japanese forces in strength within striking distance

This captured Japanese photo shows U.S. soldiers and sailors surrendering to overwhelming Japanese odds at Corregidor in the Philippines.

of Hawaii. The one-word answer was Midway. From Midway, 1,000 miles from Oahu and actually a part of the Hawaiian Archipelago, the small islands leading southeast to Oahu could be occupied and used as airfields and staging bases for the invasion.

The battle of Midway was the turning point of the war, yet it came only six months after the Pearl Harbor attack. Yamamoto's plan was to attack and occupy Midway while feinting at Alaska and launching smaller attacks in the Aleutians. He did not expect to see American carriers in the area until after Midway was secured

and the area infested with a mighty Japanese force. Japan was prepared to commit 113 surface ships and 16 submarines to the operation, and enormous quantities of fuel, which was scarce.

As far as the Japanese were concerned, the Midway invasion would spring the trap on the Pacific Fleet. What they did not know was that American code-breakers were privy to much of this planning, and the American Navy sprang a trap of its own.

Midway was assaulted by aircraft but never occupied. American aircraft from the carriers *USS Hornet, USS Yorktown,* and the *USS*

Flag raising on Iwo Jima, February 23, 1945. (Joe Rosenthal, AP.)

the 3rd Marine Division hit Agat Beach while the Army's 77th Infantry Division was landing near Apra Harbor. After five days of hard fighting the two American units joined and forced the Japanese onto Orote Peninsula. Fighting raged on inland, and on August 10 most of the organized resistance was finished, although mopping up operations continued into 1945. Some 7,300 Americans were killed or wounded; the Japanese casualties were about 18,000. Of note is that the last Japanese survivor on Guam did not surrender until 1972.

U.S. forces took back Guadalcanal in February 1943. Sitka and Kiska in the Aleutians were retaken. Tarawa and Makin fell as 1943 neared its close. In the battle of the Philippine Sea on June 19, 1944, the U.S. lost 27 airplanes but destroyed 402 aircraft. Saipan was retaken. Another 300 Japanese

Enterprise were hurled against Japanese ships and planes, and on June 5, 1942, inflicted a defeat that pushed aside all thoughts of occupying Midway and invading Hawaii. America lost the *Yorktown* to a Japanese submarine, along with a destroyer and 133 aircraft, and 320 men were killed. But the Japanese losses totaled four carriers, a heavy cruiser, and 278 aircraft, with 3,500 men killed. The Japanese pilots who went down at Midway were the best of Japan's naval aviators. No Japanese pilots afterwards would receive the same training nor approach the quality of those pilots. Midway was the first major defeat at sea for Japan, and it marked the beginning of a new era of American dominance in the vast, trackless and misnamed Pacific.

In the ensuing years Americans began to smile again. U.S forces rolled up victory after victory and some of them, such as the re-taking of Guam and Wake Island, were sweet indeed. Two weeks of Naval gunfire hammered Guam – the longest bombardment of the Pacific war – and on July 21, 1944,

General Douglas MacArthur and staff wade ashore at Leyte, in the Philippines, in October, 1944. It was a dramatic and poignant return.

CHAPTER

4

The second atomic bomb used in warfare devastated Nagasaki, Japan, sending up the now-famous mushroom cloud some 60,000 feet over the port city.

nese outright and causing the ultimate deaths of another 100,000. Three days later a second atomic bomb, "Fat Boy," devastated Nagasaki and killed 75,000 Japanese and caused injury and radiation illness to 75,000 more. On August 10, Japan sued for peace. Many Japanese heard the voice of Emperor Hirohito for the first time – on tape, declaring that Japan must "bear the unbearable." The war was over.

The man who conceived and planned the surprise attack on Pearl Harbor never lived to see Japan's final, crushing defeat. Admiral Isoroku Yamamoto, on a mission to help build morale among the various units, was being flown over the island of Bougainville on April 18, 1943, when American aircraft swarmed up and shot down his aircraft. Given choices, it probably was the death he would have preferred.

As the world watches, Japanese Foreign Minister Namoura Shigemitsu signs the surrender documents aboard the USS Missouri.

planes were destroyed on October 12, 1944, in raids on Taiwan, and a month later Allied forces invaded the Philippines.

With parallel victories in the European theatre, the end of the war in the Pacific moved closer. But fanatical Japanese militarists prepared to die to the last man – and the last woman and child. Japanese civilians were drilling with sharpened sticks, and the talk in Japan was of continued defiance.

On August 6, 1945, America dropped an atomic bomb codenamed "Little Boy" over Hiroshima, killing some 100,000 Japa-

CHAPTER FIVE

JUDGMENT

In the wake of the Pearl Harbor attack, both Admiral Kimmel and General Short were relieved of their commands and came under fire in hearings that began shortly afterwards. The first commission convened under Associate Justice of the Supreme Court Owen J. Roberts on December 22, 1941, and lasted for a month; it was the first of eight investigations, hearings or inquiries. Army and Navy officers at all levels, a range of civilians, and a handful of highly-placed government officials all underwent questioning. The War Department and the Navy Department came in for criticism. Navy Intelligence was faulted at times, exonerated at others. What emerged in the end was that the military structure from Washington to Oahu appeared to have been flawed in that full and adequate Intelligence was not shared, not shared in time, or misinterpreted. Hearings established that sweeping assumptions were made by leaders who simply neglected to pick up a telephone and make sure that everyone understood that war was imminent.

General Short's primary fault lay in his belief that the Japanese, if they were to strike at Hawaii, would do so at a time when the Pacific Fleet was away. He had reasoned that the presence of the fleet was a deterrent. Short told the Roberts Commission that he would have been extremely apprehensive if the fleet were ordered away from the Islands. Coupled with his belief that the war alert of November 27, 1941, dealt mainly with the threat of sabotage, Short's failures seemed to be matters of interpretation that he did not discuss fully with his superiors in Washington.

The war warning and other ominous developments apparently did not have the same impact on Admiral Kimmel as on other Navy officers, some in his own command. Kimmel was faulted for not committing available aircraft to reconaissance patrols north of Oahu (though other higher-ranking Navy officers agreed with that decision even in hindsight, on grounds that so few aircraft would have been ineffective and might better be marshalled for air defense).

Kimmel also felt any surprise attack would be by enemy submarines, that a torpedo attack in the harbor was impossible – not counting on the Japanese invention of fins that made low-level torpedo runs possible – and that his forces were on adequate alert. Kimmel also may have been preoccupied with War Plan Orange, the U.S. strategy for war at sea against Japan.

Kimmel would later argue that Washington had not been specific in its warnings, but this argument was brushed aside because, his detractors argued, he had failed to resolve any doubts by simply making inquiries. In the end Kimmel and Short were not held derelict in their duties, but were chastised for exercising poor judgment, and it was understood that their careers had come to an end, and not a glorious end at that.

Short and Kimmel cannot be charged with all the blame at Pearl Harbor. There was another deeper and more subtle reason for America's unpreparedness at its most important Pacific outpost. The capacity of the Japanese to attack the Hawaiian Islands was simply not taken seriously. The very audacity of the attack was a factor in its having caught the United States off-guard. U.S leadership was ready to concede that the Japanese military machine was a formidable one and could attack in any number of places. But the prospects of a Japanese attack at Pearl Harbor – while often discussed and studied in the years before the event – were somehow discounted. Through the hearings and long after, U.S. newspapers and commentators kept asking how this could happen, but the answer was obvious: American complacency in Washington and Hawaii, combined with the boldness of Japanese thinking and the precision of their planning, finally coincided. The mind-set that prevailed on the American side continued until it finally was shattered by the first bombs that fell on that bloody Sunday.

☆ ☆ ☆

CHAPTER SIX

THE JAPANESE RENAISSANCE

National Archives

General Douglas MacArthur and staff in the commander's office in the Dai Ichi Building in the heart of Tokyo.

"**M**agnanimous in victory" is a phrase often heard and seldom practiced. But because of America's magnanimity after World War II, Japan's fortunes rose from the nadir of atomic holocaust. A formal surrender ceremony took place on September 2, 1945, aboard the *USS Missouri* in Tokyo Bay, and General Douglas MacArthur was installed as Supreme Commander in Japan. Not far away Emperor Hirohito remained in the Imperial Palace, but it was the Americans who now would dictate how things were going to be, at least until the occupation ended.

How things were going to be surprised even the Japanese. A new Constitution was written that would govern Japanese affairs, and it gave the nation more of a democratic cant. The new rules forbade Japan to maintain a powerful military and set a small percentage of the budget for a self-defense force that would be too ineffectual to launch any more surprise attacks on anyone. The Americans reserved for themselves a number of bases on Japanese soil, and in a de facto arrangement Japan was scooped under the defense umbrella of the United States. Meanwhile, a steady procession of

American businesses and professionals flowed into the erstwhile enemy territory and began advising the former enemy on how to get the economy moving again. Tokyo began an extensive rebuilding program, with American help. Japanese women were given the right to vote and become a potentially strong bloc in a nation that had 73 million people. Eighty-nine women stood for election to the Diet, and 34 of them won seats.

(Interestingly, a rebuilt Tokyo was fashioned along the lines of the city as it was rebuilt following the 1923 earthquake, with houses numbered in order of their construction. As this was taking place, European cities also began their reconstruction, with Warsaw being rebuilt in part from photographs, to resemble its pre-war appearance.)

In Tokyo, one action by the occupation authorities was a mixed success. To create a more democratic and competitive business atmosphere, the Americans broke up the old *zaibatsu* – the more-or-less family companies that controlled the economy – but the familiar names continued: Mitsubishi, Mitsui, Sumitomo and others. The authorities were no less able to control social situations in which human emotions and desires proved too tough for

regulations, and there began a number of marriages between the young Americans of the occupying forces and the winsome young Japanese ladies.

Other milestones in the post-war era were duly noted. In 1949 the Japanese reparation payments were ended. Three years later the first pocket-sized transistor radios were introduced under the Sony label, not a startling development at the time but a portent of things to come. Masaru Ibuka, a Sony technician, had cut the defective rate of the transistors from 95 percent to two percent and improved the technology while lowering the cost. It was a pattern that would be repeated again and again. Only

a year later Japanese television began broadcasting, and Japan Air Lines was organized as a national overseas carrier. Clearly, the Japanese were recovering from the devastation of war.

Another indicator was auto production; in 1947 the country manufactured 110 autos, and in 1959 turned out 79,000. The production of autos seemed to focus all the Japanese traits of hard work and perseverance, and their willingness to learn and adapt. Forty years after the war, when Japan was a leading auto manufacturer and exporter, a top auto industry official summed it up for a *New York Times News Service* correspondent in Tokyo: "You came out here after the war and taught us quality control. It was a lesson we remembered and you forgot."

In the same year, 1959, Japan also produced the first transistorized television set, and went about dominating the world market. In 1964 the industrious Japanese startled the world when Tokaido Shin Kansu started service on October 1 with a "bullet" train that averaged 102 miles an hour. Eight years later the train was extended, and three years after that the line was operating on the Island of Kyushu, almost 670 miles from Tokyo.

By 1968 there was no doubting Japan's complete recovery from the war, and the statistics verified it. Its gross national product that year was $140 billion – up 12 percent – and soared past West Germany to make Japan the free world's second strongest economy, after the United States. In the same year Japan's auto production reached 21 million cars.

By the 1950s, a rapidly recovering Japan was using American assembly-line techniques and initiating strict quality control measures.

Now the heart of an expansive industrial area, Hiroshima has arisen like the proverbial phoenix, and is a city not only of wealth but of great charm.

The abilities and complexities of Japanese business were shown a few years later when Japan built and launched a supertanker of almost 477,000 tons. The Japanese trading company Mitsui had loaned 80 percent of the ship's $56 million cost to an Indian entrepreneur who chartered the supertanker back to a firm owned jointly by Japanese and American interests.

As the Japanese economy boomed, the individual Japanese began to enjoy a lifestyle hardly dreamed of earlier. The currency, the yen, increased in power dramatically, and a half-century after the attack on Pearl Harbor most Japanese were living far better than most of their former enemies. Mil-

lions of Japanese began touring the Pacific. They went to Guam, where there were heavy Japanese investments in Guam's tourist facilities. They visited obscure Pacific islands which had been the scene of bloody battles in World War II; some older Japanese went on pilgrimages to places like Guadalcanal, Saipan, and Truk. They visited islands that later made up the Trust Territories of the Pacific, under United Nations mandate but administered by the United States. (These islands attained a measure of independence toward the end of the 1980s, but America kept open the possibility of military bases in some areas, which led to disputes.)

And millions of Japanese came as visitors to Hawaii. By 1990 they made up 20 percent of the more than six million annual tourists. They had no qualms about touring Pearl Harbor and exploring the graceful memorial constructed over the hulk of the *USS Arizona*, a memorial not just to that single ship, but to all Americans who died in the December 7, 1941, attack. For some Japanese it was their first full realization of Japan's role in World War II, and it had an impact on them: a poll taken in Japan nearly 50 years after the Pearl Harbor attack showed that most young Japanese did not associate Pearl Harbor with any kind of aggression.

Their wealth pushed the Japanese to the forefront of nations providing economic aid to the rest of the world, a situation that made others – particularly the nations of South Asia – uneasy. There were few signs of Japanese militarism, but there also was no denying the strength and influence emanating from wealth. And there was no denying that Japan had reached a stage of self-sufficiency and power that would allow it to deal with the United States as an equal. A long-time U.S. Ambassador to Japan, Mike Mansfield, once remarked that the U.S.–Japanese relationship was "the most important partnership in the world today."

Fifty years after Japan's attempt to establish the Greater East Asia Co-Prosperity Sphere by military means, there were signs it was coming about peacefully. At a time when American investment in the Pacific region was $4 billion, Japan's investment was $12.5 billion. U.S. non-military aid in the Pacific totaled $139 million in 1989, compared to Japan's $4.4 billion. Noting the size of their investments and the unease it sometimes caused, Japanese officials and business began working hard at projecting a benign image. And more of them were traveling in the area: 4.6 million Japanese visited other Asian destinations in 1989, an increase of 11 percent over the previous year. Significantly, other Asians began learning Japanese as a third language, after their native tongue and English.

Still, the fears persisted in spite of Japan's ban on building an aggressive military force. Some analysts predicted that America would tire of shouldering the bur-

den of protecting Japan indefinitely, and that in time the Japanese would once again begin to assemble a military force in keeping with their economic strength. In the last half of the 1980s, at a time when the growth rate of many countries was flat, Japan spent $72 billion to modernize its defense forces. The 1990 budget alone was $28 billion, a one-year increase of six percent.

To say the Japanese lost the war that began with the rise of their militaristic factions is accurate, but that is not to say they lost their sense of competition, or purpose. In their expansionist years after the war they established economic influence over much of the world.

Japan lost the war, but as more than one historian has noted, the experience helped rid the government of the militarists who had led the nation for so long, and who might not have been stopped any other way. Thus, Japan's tactical blunder at Pearl Harbor and her ultimate defeat may have been the only way for the nation to be set on a course of peace and prosperity that has led Japan to a position of dominance today.

In the long view of history, Japan suffered terrible losses, but in the end, prevailed.

☆ ☆ ☆

Embassy of Japan

Japanese technology has taken a leading world role; at this university, atomic research is being pursued as these researchers investigate a heavy ion beam.

CHAPTER SEVEN

THE TURBULENT DECADES

United Nations

Flags bedeck the final home of the United Nations, at Lake Success New York. Flawed and sometimes ineffectual, the UN nevertheless became a positive symbol of man's continuing search for order.

While Japan was preoccupied with rebuilding, the United States was busily standing down its military and turning to the complexities of peace as it was being defined in a post-war world. In a sense the attack on Pearl Harbor and the American prosecution of the war to its successful outcome marked the end of an era in which nations could talk or fight more or less alone. No longer could any nation operate in a vacuum, and long before the word "ecology" would become popular, there was a global ecology developing that once arrived would never depart. In the wake of World War II, the next decades were to prove both fascinating and turbulent.

As events tumbled upon each other, and as both Washington and Tokyo reacted to those events, there were subtle shifts in outlook. At some point after World War II, both American and Japanese leadership began to devote as much time and energy to foreign affairs as they did to domestic ones, for in the wake of war there were new channels of communications and transportation. Foreign products began to reach American markets with growing rapidity; often they were better products than could be found at home. Simultaneously, America exported not only its wares but its ways of doing things. American knowledge and methods at all levels went out to friends and former foes.

Because of increasing American involvement in international business and commerce, and because trade was a fact of life that now needed to be refined, America busied itself with events overseas in a way it had never done before. Instead of talk of a "Fortress America", there was growing concern with other nations' problems. Long after the end of World War II, President John F. Kennedy

Tons of water and sand are thrown aloft by an atomic bomb test at Bikini Atoll in the Marshall Islands in 1947.

would articulate what already was in practice – that the United States would "bear any burden" to assist the cause of freedom around the world, that while one man was enslaved, no man was free. It was a growing philosophy that shaped post-war thinking, and like all movements it had its good and bad aspects. Some Americans felt the United States was too concerned with being its brother's keeper.

Nevertheless, American news-papers now devoted more space to occurrences abroad. It became clear that the vast geopolitical eco-system meant that a man with a gun in Jordan could cause ripples in Washington, Tokyo, London, Paris, Nairobi, and elsewhere around the globe. Suddenly, any event, anywhere, might have an international impact.

It was a vast misconception if America thought the combat was over. Hardly had World War II ended when there was a percep-tible shifting of gears, and one of the major players of World War II began to do the unthinkable: a nation that had fought for free-dom began to hold its own people in captivity. As usual, it was Win-ston Churchill who phrased it best: "From Stettin in the Baltic to Tri-este in the Adriatic, an iron cur-tain has descended across the Con-tinent." The Russians had begun what was one of the most pro-found and pivotal situations of the post-war era, the Cold War. With frightening efficiency the So-viets kept their own people inside the boundaries, and others out. Communism descended on the Eastern Bloc countries with a ven-geance, religion was abolished, in-dividuals were subordinated to the State, and the Russian government entered its most xenophobic stage. The threat seemed unmistakable, and America continued to react to that threat: U.S. military forces began testing atomic weapons at an obscure atoll in the Marshall Islands called Bikini.

There was reaction on the dip-lomatic front as well. The United Nations General Assembly opened its first session on January 10, 1946 in London, with Paul Spaak of Belgium as president. Seven days later the U.N. Security Council met in London and named Norwegian Socialist Trygve Lie as its first Sec-retary-General. On December 14, the United Nations accepted a gift of $8.5 million from John D. Rock-erfeller, Jr., to buy property in Turtle Bay, on New York's East River, for a permanent headquarters.

One of the ugliest of man's memorials was the Berlin Wall, which separated East and West Germany. With reunification this grim barrier, shown here under construction, was torn down.

Still the war was fresh in the mind, for on September 30 of that year the Nuremberg Tribunal returned death sentences against 12 leading Nazis, along with a number of lesser sentences and a few acquittals.

In the next months, while Tokyo was being rebuilt, world powers signed a far-ranging General Agreement on Tariffs and Trade (GATT). It was designed to lower tariff barriers and help world trade. Simultaneously, the United States was about to embark on another far-ranging world economic plan by proposing financial aid to European countries willing to assist in the task of recovery. It would be known as the Marshall Plan.

The Marshall Plan was implemented in 1948, a year in which Hindu extremists assassinated Mahatma Gandhi because they resented his agreement to the partition of India and Pakistan. It was also the year that the nation of Israel came into being, and the Olympic games were held for the first time since 1936. The Soviets, however, reminded the world of their strength when occupation forces in Germany set up a blockade on July 24 to cut rail and highway traffic between West Germany and Berlin. The U.S. response was swift and effective: the following day U.S. and British aircraft began flying in food and supplies to the more than two million

people of West Berlin, reaching 4,500 tons of supplies a day and keeping it up until September of 1949. Still in 1948, implementation of the Marshall Plan saw an authorization of $5.3 billion for economic aid to 16 European countries, and it was apparent that the Cold War meant that the United States and the Soviet Bloc were going to compete in every way short of total war.

The very thought of war led to ominous developments. America intensified its atomic testing in the Pacific, and on April 4, joined Canada, Iceland, Britain, France, Denmark, Norway, Belgium, the Netherlands, Luxembourg, Italy, and Portugal in a pledge of mutual

A sign of the times that would change: Mikhail Gorbachev's glastnost (openness) would bring down the Berlin Wall and signs like these.

assistance against aggression, a grouping they called the North Atlantic Treaty Organization (NATO). The Russians retaliated with a similar entity called the Warsaw Pact. The Soviets also believed they had an ally in the new People's Republic of China, a Communist country whose forces had chased General Chiang Kaishek and his Kuomintang troops to the off-shore island of Taiwan.

The U.S. watched the instability in Asia with a growing disquiet, but still was caught off-balance when North Korea invaded South Korea on June 25, 1950. From its bases in Japan, the United States began to funnel troops and supplies to the aid of beleaguered South Korean forces and a war was on in earnest. There was a difference this time: allied forces in Korea were fighting under a new banner, the flag of the United Nations. And for a time the war seemed to be going the U.N.'s way. But on December 28, Chinese Communists entered the war, thus prolonging it until an armistice was signed late in July 1953. Historians noted it was merely an armistice; technically the war had not ended by 1990.

The Chinese intervention in Korea took place at the same time other Chinese Communist units were invading and occupying Tibet. U.S. President Harry S. Truman was authorizing the development of the hydrogen bomb, and the Russians were announcing that they, too, had an atomic bomb. The world population now stood at 2.52 billion, and it is unlikely that anyone felt comfortable with the tensions extant in the world at the time.

In the early stages of the Korean War the United States and Japan entered a partnership that was unthinkable a short six years earlier: on September 8, 1951, they signed a mutual security pact. This pact permitted American troops to remain in Japan indefinitely to assist U.N. operations in Asia, and no other nation was permitted to have bases in Japan without American consent.

One of the lucky ones, an escapee from East Berlin is helped from a tunnel underneath the famous Berlin Wall.

The death of Soviet leader Josef Stalin in 1953 brought no easing of tensions; instead it introduced a succession of rulers who differed only in style and did not deviate from the relentless pursuit of the Cold War. The Iron Curtain seemed as impenetrable as ever. Unrest continued across Asia as well. The United States recognized Vietnam's independence, the Korean War came to its stalemated truce talks phase, the French suffered a crushing defeat by Viet Minh forces at Dien Bien Phu, and it seemed that overnight there was civil war in Vietnam.

In 1957 the Soviet Union launched its Sputnik I, triggering two disparate reactions. Scientists hailed the achievement as opening new frontiers of study, while professional soldiers began to ponder the terrifying new possibilities of war from outer space. America scrambled to catch up in the space race, with varying degrees of success. The United Kingdom, meanwhile, tested its own atomic bomb at Christmas Island in the Pacific, and was soon followed by the French, whose own tests at Mururoa, southeast of Tahiti, would continue long after other nations had stopped.

The decade of the 1960s brought little improvement to the relationships that counted among those fervently hoping for an end to the Cold War. On August 15, 1961, a wall was erected between East and West Berlin that stopped all movement from one to the other. The Berlin Wall was a direct response to a Warsaw Pact request to end the mass exodus of East Berliners to the West. Now the Iron Curtain had a tangible symbol, and one that pleased the Soviets as representative of their power.

Less thrilling to the Soviets was the sharp break between Russia and the People's Republic of China, a division in the ranks of the two top Communist nations that would continue for almost 30 years.

A year later the world's worst fears seemed about to be confirmed when President Kennedy came face-to-face with Russia's Nikita Khrushchev over the issue of missiles in Cuba. It was a nuclear confrontation of the kind the world had worried about from the advent of atomic weaponry, and the American reaction was a "quaran-

Brig. Gen. Courtney Whitney; Gen. Douglas MacArthur, Commander in Chief of U.N. Forces; and Maj. Gen. Edward M. Almond observe the shelling of Inchon from the USS Mt. McKinley, September 15, 1950.

CHAPTER

7

A gun crew aims and fires a 75mm recoilless rifle near Oetlook-tong, Korea in 1951, a year of some of the hardest fighting of the war.

tine" of Cuba via naval blockade. Once again America appeared to be on the brink of war, as Khrushchev remained stubborn, and demanded the U.S withdrawal of missiles from their bases in Turkey as a quid-pro-quo for dismantling the Cuban missiles. Kennedy rejected the plan. In time, Khrushchev agreed to dismantle the missile sites, and U.S. missiles in Turkey eventually were quietly removed. There was a national – perhaps international – sigh of relief.

It probably was the young president's finest hour, but he did not enjoy it for long. On November 22, 1963, Kennedy was assassinated in a motorcade in Dallas. Lee Harvey Oswald was arrested and was, in turn, killed by a gun fired by nightclub owner Jack Ruby as millions watched on television.

Kennedy's death had been preceded by the assassination in Vietnam of South Vietnam's Ngo Dinh Diem, in a coup that some claimed was engineered by the United States. The civil war in Vietnam intensified.

Twenty years after the end of World War II there seemed to be as much unrest and confusion in the world as at any previous time. Significantly, Japan stood aside from much of it, engrossed instead in major expansion of its industry. In a year that saw Congress approve the Tonkin Gulf resolution, taking the U.S. deeper into the Vietnam quagmire; the death of India's Nehru; the expansion of apartheid in South Africa; Saudi Arabia's Saud ibn Abdel Azia deposed; a coup in Brazil; the segue of Northern Rhodesia into the new nation of Zambia; creation of the new United Republic of Tanganyika; and even the ouster of Khrushchev in favor of Leonid Brezhenev – in

that same year the largest iron ore contract in history began supplying Japan's major steel firms with 65.5 million tons of ore. Over the next 20 years the use of that iron, supplied by Australia with the backing of several nations including the United States, brought about the expansion of the Japanese steel industry and helped make that nation a new industrial superpower.

In the United States it was, to invoke Dickens, "the best of times... the worst of times." There were phenomenal advances in science and medicine, in literature and art, in transportation and communications. There were triumphs, such as the electric moment on July 21, 1969, when Neil Armstrong stepped from the lunar module of Apollo 11 and put his foot on the surface of the moon. "One small step for man," he said, "one giant step for mankind."

But there were tragedies. Robert Kennedy, brother of the slain John F. Kennedy, was himself killed in a hail of bullets on June 5, 1968, in the kitchen pantry of a Los Angeles hotel. Jordanian-American Sirhan Bishara Sirhan, 24, was arrested and convicted of Kennedy's murder. Only the previous April 4, civil rights leader Martin Luther King, Jr., was killed by a single shot from a 30.06 Remington rifle. Arrested, convicted, and sentenced to 99 years in prison was ex-convict James Earl Ray. King's death caused race riots in which 46 people were killed and almost 22,000 were arrested.

The tragedies mounted. In the same year, My Lai village in South Vietnam was the scene of a massa-

On a raw day that matched the nation's mood, President Kennedy's funeral procession took the President on his last journey.

cre on March 16, as U.S. troops killed scores of non-combatant villagers. The news was suppressed for almost two years, but eventually the blame fell on Army First Lieutenant William Calley, Jr. The story of the massacre intensified anti-war protests in the United States, renewing calls to pull U.S. forces out of Vietnam. The Americans had been in Vietnam since the early 1960s, and as the months and years went by the war proved to be as wrenching as anything in America's history since the Civil War. As in that period, families were divided in their loyalty.

In 1965 there were 125,000 American troops in Vietnam, and by 1968, the year of the My Lai massacre, a peak of 550,000 was

It was a time when the whole world held its breath, and the news was tragic: JFK Is Shot In Dallas. Another American President had fallen victim to an assassin's bullet.

reached. As in any war, many of them were support personnel, but a significant number of young Americans were involved in a war that was terrifying, shadowy, deadly, and enervating. It began with American advisors to South Vietnamese forces and ended with Americans in the front lines. It began with guerilla tactics and small-unit, jungle warfare and ended with set-piece battles and tank operations. In 1968 the Tet holiday offensive by the Viet Cong and North Vietnamese Army triggered another wave of protest across the United States, for while they suffered terrible losses, the enemy's action aroused the American public to a fever pitch of protest. And even the protests carried the seeds of tragedy: on May 4, 1970 students of Kent State University in Ohio rallied to protest the expanding war. They were fired on by National Guardsmen who killed four and wounded eight others, setting off a firestorm of additional protest. Five days later at least 75,000 people demonstrated in Washington D.C. against the war, and an embattled President Richard M. Nixon drove to the Lincoln Memorial before dawn to talk for an hour with the protesters.

The divisive war took its toll on those supporting it, those fighting it, and those protesting it. By the time American forces pulled out of Vietnam in 1973, following Nixon's policy of "Vietnamization" of the war, some 55,000 Americans had died in the jungles and paddies and treacherous village streets and paths. And, as many had predicted, with the departure of the Americans South Vietnam

South Vietnam's Chairman Nguyen Van Thieu, President Johnson, South Vietnam's Prime Minister Nguyen Cao Ky, and assistants salute during the national anthems of both nations at a wartime meeting in Guam.

fell to the armies of the North, and a reign of terror began. South Vietnamese officers were placed in "re-education camps" which were little more than concentration camps. Families were broken up, with men disappearing never to be seen again. And while the North proved adept at prosecuting the war, nearly 20 years after it had ended, the economy of the Socialist Republic of Vietnam remained in a shambles.

Years after the war ended the bitterness continued. America's young men had fought gallantly in the jungles and paddies of Southeast Asia, then had come home to a nation which tended to confuse the men with the war itself. Throughout the months and years the Vietnam veterans were reviled by a large segment of the public which had elected the officials which sent men to war. Long years later, when some of the public hysteria had died down, the American public began to appreciate the sacrifices of the Vietnam veterans.

For many veterans the long-delayed acceptance left a residue of bitterness they would take to their graves.

Throughout those years a steady stream of refugees poured out of Vietnam, many of them coming to the United States, and a lesser but still significant number ending up in Japan. The exodus was primarily by sea, as thousands of Vietnamese crowded into rickety boats and pushed off into unfriendly seas. They were drowned in storms, raped and killed by Thai pirates, and washed up on beaches where the natives pushed them unceremoniously back out to sea. They had used most, if not all, of their funds to bribe their way past sentries and to buy space on the dangerously overcrowded and frail craft, and when they did gain at least temporary acceptance in Malaysia, Thailand, or Hong Kong, they still were resented for causing problems.

When the first mass exodus occurred, the attitudes of Americans

CHAPTER

7

Far from home, a U.S. astronaut stands before the flag of his country amid a barren moonscape; the U.S. achievement electrified the world.

Viet Cong prisoners await evacuation by helicopter after a Marine sweep south of Chu Lai, Vietnam, in August of 1965.

did not bode well for the future of the refugees. America's long and frustrating involvement in Vietnam may have been partly responsible for the results of a Gallup poll in May 1975 that indicated Americans were opposed to admitting Vietnamese refugees by 54 to 36 percent. Against some opposition, Congress designed new refugee legislation on May 22, 1975, appropriating funds to assist refugees. As years went by, however, and the refugees seemed to keep coming, the United States and most other nations tightened their borders against the influx, contending that later arrivals were not refugees but "illegal immigrants" looking for better prospects. Compounding the problem was the flight of some two million Cambodians, fleeing first the "killing fields" of the Communist Khmer Rouge, then the invasion of the Vietnamese. Thousands of Cambodians ended up in refugee camps on the Thai-Cambodian border, and in 1990 thousands were still there.

Other events demanded America's attention. President Nixon made a historic visit to China, a trip that observers thought might open the country to more progressive thought – and for a while, seemed to. Nixon became the first U.S. President to visit Moscow. Then he crashed on the shoals of Watergate. At 2 a.m. on June 17, 1972, five men were arrested inside Democratic Party headquarters at the Watergate apartment complex in Washington D.C., and reporters began tracing the rationale behind the break-in to politics that implicated the White House. Eventually, Nixon bowed to pressure and became the first and only U.S. president to resign.

While these developments were making news, other events competed for space on Page One: Vice President Spiro Agnew resigned on October 10, 1973, after being charged with income tax evasion.

The touch of human hands, East to West, meant the end to an era of separation as the two German states became one republic.

Symbol of a new era, a national flag goes up over a reunited Germany.

U.S. troops finally left Vietnam in a messy evacuation from Saigon. An oil crisis gripped the nation and the world following an Arab oil embargo, followed by soaring grain prices which triggered a monetary crisis – and a subsequent worldwide economic recession, the worst since the Great Depression of the 1930s.

Almost overlooked in these rapid-fire developments was a quiet ceremony in 1972 in which the United States returned Okinawa, scene of some of the bloodiest fighting in World War II, to the Japanese.

The 1980s began what military men privately called "the dangerous decade." There was no apparent end to the Cold War, and the nuclear club had expanded to include China and (it was speculated) India, which apparently tested a nuclear device in the Rajasthan Desert in 1974. The arms buildup continued unabated and America underwent a recession in the early 1980s, not as severe as the one in 1973, but damaging enough. The mood in America probably could best be described as restless. As Japan's economy boomed, the American economy tended to go up and down, affecting different sections of the country. A strong environmentalist trend gathered strength in the United States, and often the proponents of more jobs found themselves in conflict with the advocates of saving the environment.

In other events, India's Prime Minister Indira Gandhi was gunned down by her own bodyguards

President Reagan and Chairman Gorbachev face each other flanked by aides as they begin a U.S.-Soviet summit meeting in Moscow. Reagan's "evil empire" rhetoric faded as his friendship with Gorbachev developed.

in New Delhi; "Ninoy" Aquino was assassinated as he arrived back in the Philippines to contest for leadership, and in the furor that followed Ferdinand Marcos (who had established an apparent perpetual martial law) was forced to flee the country; Egypt's Anwar Sadat, who made a courageous journey to Israel to solidify new and peaceful relations between Israelis and Arabs, later was killed in a hail of gunfire; aircraft hijackings became almost commonplace; Pakistan's leader, General Zia, was killed when a bomb exploded on his airplane; and in the Middle East, various terrorist groups began taking hostages. It was a year-long hostage crisis culminated by a failed rescue effort by U.S. forces in the Iranian desert that cost President Jimmy Carter his re-election.

The decade proved dangerous enough, but as it neared an end there were developments that would startle the world.

A phenomenon named Mikhail Gorbachev was waiting in the wings of Russia. His ascent to power in the Soviet Union gave rise to speculation that in the end would pale beside the reality of the changes he would bring, not only to the Soviet Union but to the world. There was, perhaps, a clue in the words of England's Prime Minister Margaret Thatcher after her first meeting with the new Soviet General Secretary: "He's a man we can work with." The sweeping nature of Gorbachev's reforms were hidden at first, but gradually the world began to notice that here was a Soviet leader remarkably free of dogma, apparently willing to abandon old practices and fears, and embark in new directions.

Hope began to grow, then to blossom. Gorbachev was inclined more to improve the Russian economy than its war machine; he brought Soviet forces home from Afghanistan. Ironically, the Russian citizenry used its new-found freedom under Gorbachev to complain he was not improving the economy fast enough! Systematically, Gorbachev began to dismantle the ponderous Politburo thinking, and the world was treated to a startling series of events.

On November 9, 1989, the Berlin Wall began to crumble under the onslaught of Germans who felt free enough to destroy it. Bits of it went as souvenirs, and whole massive slabs of this ugly symbol lay in rubbish dumps in a now undivided city of Berlin. East and West Germans mingled freely and laid plans for reunification. Other monoliths fell as well: in Romania the government was over-

The Man of the Hour, Mikhail Gorbachev talks with Germans on the eve of reunification. The Soviet leader's popularity alternately rocketed and plummeted against a backdrop of unrest in his own Soviet Union.

turned, its leadership executed. In the Baltic, the Russian satellites of Latvia, Lithuania, and Estonia began the road back to self-determination. Poland and Hungary underwent democratic reorganizations and looked to free elections. At midnight on October 3, 1990, the black, red, and gold flag of a unified Germany rose in front of a floodlit Reichstag in Berlin, heralding the fact of one Germany, united for the first time in 41 years.

At the same time, the West and the Soviet Bloc agreed to massive cuts in both NATO and Warsaw Pact forces. Negotiators agreed on a balance of power in tanks, artillery, armored combat vehicles, aircraft, and troops. In a development just as astonishing to the postwar generation, the Soviet Parliament passed a new "Law on Freedom of Conscience" by a vote of

A student leader of the Chinese demonstrations in May, 1989, Wu'er Kaixi is attended to in Tiananmen Square during a hunger strike to protest government restrictions. His real name, Uerkesh Daolet, reflected his Uigar minority background, but he became the symbol of the student movement.

52

341 to 2, a law that allowed the return of religious freedom to Russia. The law affected an estimated 131 million Russians who had maintained their faith through the long years of religious oppression. Their faith was obviously justified. Wire service photos carried a picture of former KGB General Oleg Kalugin, lighting a candle in St. Basil's Cathedral in the heart of Moscow.

Then, among 15 constituent republics of the U.S.S.R., some also began a call for self-determination. There would be a measure of it, enough to warrant a new treaty of confederation. It would even initiate a debate in the Russian government about whether, with all the changes, the Union of Soviet Socialist Republic ought to have a new name.

In China, a group of tired old men suddenly cracked down on democratic impulses, and in June 1989, Chinese soldiers killed dem-

John Schidlovsky

Chinese students in Beijing have their brief moment in the sun in May, 1989, as pro-democracy movements consolidated and demanded new freedoms. Here a hunger strike by movement leaders is supported by masses, but in the end the Chinese hard-liners prevailed and the students were routed, suffering reprisals.

CHAPTER

7

A GI returning home to Hawaii from the Gulf War shows the remarkable patriotism that the war engendered, both at home and in ranks of the military.

onstrators in Tiananmen Square in the heart of Beijing; the leadership under Deng Xiaoping pulled China back into its shell.

But all across the map of Eastern Europe the massive changes had a common theme: it was apparent that the Communist system did not work, and even the Russians were abandoning it for some more efficient, democratic process.

The Cold War, thanks to the personal efforts of Mikhail Gorbachev (who won a Nobel Peace Prize in 1990 for his efforts), had segued into something else. Rela-

tionships with the West certainly were better than they had ever been, but Gorbachev had problems at home: the various states of the Russian federation were seeking their own independence and some Russian Army units reacted with violence. With Russia itself in turmoil, the world held its breath.

When the next shooting war came, World War II was historic, not personal; in 1991 only 30 percent of the nation's 250 million people were alive at the end of World War II, so for two-thirds of Americans, the war in the desert

became the first war the U.S. had won. Korea was a draw, Vietnam a loss, but what became known as the Gulf War was a resounding victory.

The Gulf War began with the movement of Iraqi troops into neighboring Kuwait, and the subsequent claiming of that oil-rich nation as another province of Iraq. Iraq's leader, Saddam Hussein, refused all pleas to pull his forces back and leave Kuwait to its independence, and the United Nations passed resolutions urging withdrawal. Promising "the mother of all battles," Saddam Hussein re-

Official Department of Defense photo by R. D. Ward

At a post-Gulf war session, the architects of an allied victory meet in Washington: General Norman Schwartzkopf, Defense Secretary Dick Cheney, President George Bush and General Colin Powell, Chairman of the Joint Chiefs of Staff.

jected the resolutions and moved massive units of men and armor into the Kuwaiti desert area near the border of Saudi Arabia. America reacted – proving that the global ecology was alive and well – by giving Iraq a deadline of January 15, 1991, to get out of Kuwait, and spearheading a coalition of 28 nations who sent troops and equipment to Saudi Arabia in anticipation of Iraq's determination to fight.

On January 17, American and coalition forces began a massive air assault on Iraqi positions in Kuwait and in Iraq itself. On February 24, the coalition began a ground offensive that in just 100 hours rolled the Iraqis back, liberated Kuwait, and took huge numbers of Iraqi prisoners. In the full 43 days of the air war and ground offensive, 149 were killed and 513 wounded from the coalition, while Iraq suffered at least 100,000 dead and wounded.

The Gulf War was a violent expression of the changes taking place in the Middle East. Palestinians were demanding a homeland, Israel was demanding relief from Arab terrorism, and the United States and its partners in the successful coalition were talking about a new world order that would put an end to terrorism and launch the world into a new time of peace. The only certainty was that there would continue to be change and evolution.

☆ ☆ ☆

Joint PAO, MCAS, Kaneohe Bay

The Gulf War was mercifully short, and the celebrations that began almost immediately continued for months. For the returning GIs, the real celebration was reunion with loved ones.

CHAPTER EIGHT

TO REMEMBER PEARL HARBOR

Official U.S. Navy Photograph

For many, Pearl Harbor is remembered in photos such as this one, or in histories; the four men here, however, were there at the time. Now volunteers at the USS Arizona Memorial, left to right are Bill Speer, Warren Verhoff, Art Critchett and Joe Morgan.

Official U.S. Navy Photograph

Among the Americans who had survived that bloody Sunday, some came back to Hawaii to stay. They noted the massive changes that seemed to come quickly and continually to Hawaii, but they also noted that Pearl Harbor had remained pretty much the same five decades after the bombing. Joe Morgan was aware of a few new buildings on Ford Island, but the look and feel

Bill Speer, fifth from left, photographed over 40 years after the Pearl Harbor attack in a group that contained six former Jap–anese pilots who participated in the raid.

of it was similar to that morning long ago when he stood in a hangar, waiting to muster with the rest of Utility Squadron Two. He was 19 then, a high school dropout from Tyler, Texas. Morgan heard the droning of aircraft engines and assumed a mock attack, a training exercise, was underway. Then the first bomb fell among a group of patrol planes. He and others ran outside and saw the second dive-bomber climbing upward, the rising sun insignia on its wings.

"It was a total, complete surprise," he recalled. "We knew there were negotiations going on in Washington between the U.S. and Japan. We were even on an alert. But nobody expected this." Morgan climbed into the waist-hatch of a PBY patrol aircraft and manned the 30-caliber machine gun. For 45 long minutes he fired at airplanes flashing overhead, hitting a lot of them but never knowing if he brought any down. He remembered one plane in flames, and the pilot turning it deliberately into the USS Curtiss.

That night Morgan made his commitment to God. Three months later he married the local girl he had been seeing, and spent much of the war at the Naval Air Station at Puunene, on the Island of Maui. Afterward he went to the seminary and became a Baptist minister, eventually getting his Doctor of Ministry degree – a long way from the dropout he had once been. Morgan also stayed in the Navy Reserve and was back on active duty for the Vietnam conflict. For awhile he was pastor of the Wailuku Baptist Church in Wailuku, Maui, then pastor at the

Carl Shaneff

The flag flies proudly above the Arizona Memorial, a memorial to all who fell that Sunday morning. The site is one of the most revered of American military memorials.

Bill Speer in uniform of 1941. These were later changed for protection against burns.

Aina Haina Baptist Church on Oahu. Fifty years after the attack, Morgan was the volunteer chaplain for the Arizona, where he took part in ceremonies, and was available for invocations, benedictions, and funerals.

It was on Maui that Morgan met one of the Pearl Harbor attackers in person. It was none other than Mitsuo Fuchida, leader of the attack and now a Protestant minister who had been converted to Christianity simply by reading the Bible. Morgan recalled Fuchida as "an impressive man, quite intelligent." He thought Fuchida a bit sensitive to any ill feelings Americans might have harbored. "He had a genuine commitment to God," Morgan remembered, "and he seemed a little put out that some people might still have some animosity toward him. There was no animosity in my own heart; God had erased it."

Another 19-year-old that Sunday was Art Critchett, part of the deck force of the *USS Dewey*, situated in a nest of other destroyers moored with a mother ship 200

yards off the north end of Ford Island. Critchett was sitting on the destroyer's fantail reading a newspaper when the airplanes roared overhead. He went quickly to his general quarters station in the Number Three five-inch gun on the ship's aft section. However, his gun could not operate since most of the ship's ammunition was ashore during its overhaul period. There was only one operational five-inch gun on the ship, and about all Critchett could do was look around in fright. What he saw was still vivid in his mind. When the havoc ended the *Dewey's* engine room gang had the ship ready for sea, and she left harbor at 3 p.m. to take up a patrol sweep off Oahu. The only damage the ship suffered had been to a radio antenna, when another U.S. destroyer rocked into it from the force of a bomb explosion. At sea the ship came upon a large naval force and steamed forward to challenge it; the "enemy" turned out to be the *USS Enterprise* and her accompanying ships returning from Wake Island.

In August 1943, Critchett encountered the enemy once again when his ship the *USS Lipscomb Bay* was torpedoed and sunk off Makin Island. Critchett was among the 250-odd survivors out of the 1,000-man crew. He knew he had been lucky twice. In 1961 he retired from the Navy after a career as a Hospitalman. He took a federal job as a quarantine inspector along the Mexican border, later working for the California Department of Corrections.

In March 1986, Critchett came home to Hawaii, and found that everything in the Islands had changed except Pearl Harbor,

Carl Shaneff

Sailors from today's Navy in front of the memorial wall that lists the names of those lost in the USS Arizona. This memorial room functions as a place for ceremony & remembrance.

A view from the interior of Arizona Memorial. Structurally sound and highly symbolic, the memorial has been seen by millions of visitors.

where the immensity of the base seemed to mask the changes. There was a new Naval Supply building and other construction, but time seemed to have paused over the huge harbor.

Bill Speer was no teenager at the time of the attack. He was an older man of 23, Kentucky-born, a career man who was already a Yeoman Second Class, assigned to the light cruiser *USS Honolulu*. The opening moments of the war caught him literally with his pants down; he was en route from a shower and was wearing only his skivvies when the first bombs fell. Speer went directly to his general quarters station as a telephone talker. He and the ship both escaped direct hits that morning, but a bomb tore through the dock alongside and exploded beneath it. The blast ruptured the Hono–lulu's seams and she began taking on sea water. When he saw the devastation around him, Speer counted himself and his shipmates lucky.

Speer stayed in the Navy as he had intended to do all along, and retired as a Chief Yeoman. Along the way he served temporarily as an Ensign, and in accordance with Navy regulations, drew an Ensign's retirement pay. He worked for a time in California but returned to Hawaii in 1980, and like others, found many changes. Pearl Harbor, though, seemed not too different. Speer found a personal crusade when he realized that American textbooks gave too little attention to America's wars, in his opinion. (One textbook had two pages on all U.S. wars, and seven pages on the entertainment industry). Now Speer, a volunteer at the National Park at Pearl Harbor, used every opportunity to educate young people about the attack, the war, and subsequent events that impacted strongly on a whole generation of Americans.

Education is one of the goals of the Pearl Harbor Survivors Association, a group of some 11,000 persons who were on active duty on Oahu or within a three-mile radius during the attack. The local segment of that group, the Aloha Chapter, was headed 50 years later by Don Howell, who said that educational programs about the attack and programs designed to help people remember

The submarine USS Bowfin, today a memorial, in its wartime missions proved to be one of the more effective - and colorful - undersea boats.

Pearl Harbor are objectives of the group, along with the fellowship of those who survived the surprise attack.

Howell was a 21-year old recruit trainee at Schofield Barracks who happened to be at his home in Nuuanu when the attack began. He hitched a ride to town and linked up with other soldiers who were being taxied back to Schofield. They passed by Pearl Harbor and were astonished at the violence. When they reached Schofield they found the expected confusion, but soon were issued small arms and ammunition. Some of the raw recruits were assigned to guard duty at various posts. Later, Howell was assigned to guard some of the Japanese and German detainees at Sand Island, many of whom were shipped to camps on the U.S. mainland. Among the German detainees was Howell's boss–the man he worked for at the firm of Von-Hamm Young & Associates. It was, Howell recalled, about as awkward as it could get.

Howell spent much of the war in various ordinance jobs, putting in a little more than four years before taking his discharge as a Technical Sergeant in 1945. He returned to Von-Hamm Young, segued into the insurance division and later worked for Amfac, and still later for the Fireman's Fund. He retired in 1985, and began to devote much of his time to the Pearl Harbor Survivor's Association. The Association has chapters in each state, 39 of which issue special license plates (although not Hawaii, as of this writing).

Like other survivors, Howell agreed that the attack was a surprise, and that Americans were caught unprepared. He took it a step further: "Americans can," he said, "be proud of the way U.S. forces reacted that day." He remembers some initial confusion, but he also remembers an undercurrent of anger that seemed to motivate the soldiers and sailors on Oahu to react with determination.

It was that high moral outrage and the shock of the attack that in the end united Americans, becoming a part of the equipment that Americans carried through the long and costly war, a war that ended as some Japanese strategists feared it would – in an American victory.

There is a memorial at Pearl Harbor that contains a plaque for each of the 52 submarines and nearly 4,000 submariners the United States lost in the war. The Submarine Memorial is a place of quiet contemplation at its best moments. Also at Pearl Harbor is the USS Bowfin (SS 287) at Bowfin Park, maintained as a memorial to the lost submarines and their crews.

But it is the memorial alongside Ford Island that is a magnet for visitors. Its simple and graceful design is long-lasting and highly symbolic. It is a memorial that came into being only after considerable controversy and a lot of help from interested citizens.

No one is sure who first suggested a memorial remembering the attack, but at least one civilian worker at the Pearl Harbor Naval Shipyard advanced plans and ideas as early as 1943. In 1949 the Territory of Hawaii established a Pacific War Memorial Commis-

Carl Shaneff

A ribbon of oil still leaks from the sunken hulk of the USS Arizona; this photo taken from the memorial, shows the section of the battleship just above the waterline.

61

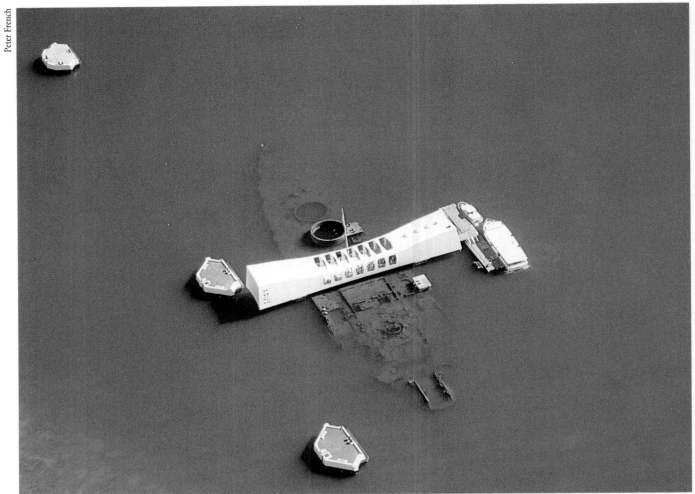

Outline of the USS Arizona shows through the waters of Pearl Harbor, a reminder of the terrible price of war. Above the hulk, the pristine memorial is a symbol that the sacrifices are not forgotten.

sion, whose chairman, business-man and former Navy Officer Tucker Gratz, had thought of such a memorial in 1946. On March 7, 1950, the Pacific Fleet's Com-mander-in-Chief, Admiral Arthur Radford, ordered a flagstaff in-stalled on the protruding hulk of the *USS Arizona*, the flag to be raised and lowered daily. In time a wooden platform was added. Na-tionally, there was interest in a memorial and Congressman Tho-mas Lane of Massachusetts intro-

Known as the Arizona Memorial, this graceful and symbolic structure next to Ford Island is a memorial to all Americans who fell on that fateful Sunday.

duced bills in 1950 and 1951 authorizing a shrine at the Arizona site.

Various factions wanted the memorial, but for different reasons, and about the same time it became obvious that fund-raising efforts would be long and arduous. The Navy Club was enthusiastic, but unable to raise sufficient funds. It would take an act of Congress to allow the Navy to accept funds for construction from the Pacific War Memorial Commission, and from there the problem degenerated into a bureaucratic nightmare. It was Hawaii's delegate to Congress (and later Governor) John A. Burns who arranged a way out – any funds except federal funding could be accepted for the memorial. This paved the way for private donations. Meanwhile, the American Battle Monuments Commission was wary of intrusions into its domain, but finally legal authorization was obtained for fund-raising.

Various fund-raisers entered the scene, some more effective than others. A December 3, 1958, broadcast of the "This Is Your Life" television program hosted by Ralph Edwards raised more than $95,000 for the memorial. The Hawaii legislature appropriated $50,000 in 1959 and added another $50,000 in 1961 when Texas Congressman Olin Teague promised congressional appropriations if there was a shortfall. The editor of the Honolulu Advertiser, George Chaplin, wrote some 1,500 letters to newspaper editors across the nation, asking them to publicize the need for funds. The publicity drew a response from rock star Elvis Presley, who performed in Hawaii on March 25, 1961, raising

another $64,696 for the cause.

Despite an initial understanding that no federal monies would be involved in the memorial, and despite disapproval of some Congressmen because of that understanding, Congress eventually set aside $150,000 to aid in the memorial's construction. There were to be other negative notes sounded during the efforts to make the memorial a reality, but in time the funds were in hand, and in August 1959, Alfred Preis of a Honolulu architectural firm was picked to design the memorial.

Preis' first design was unacceptable to the Navy, but his next one incorporated a soaring, pleasing effect that reminded visitors of the sacrifices made, and the price of victory. While the design was utilitarian and workable, it also was highly symbolic.

The rise of the memorial at the end of the pier represents the strength of the United States prior to the Pearl Harbor attack, while the dip in the center signifies the dark days of the tragedy suffered on December 7, 1941. The rise of the memorial at its other end symbolizes the ultimate victory of the United States and the end of World War II. Seven windows on each side and the seven windows on the top in the center represent a perpetual 21-gun salute. The memorial houses three sections, displaying plaques and museum artifacts and the

names of the more than 1,000 men who died with the battleship.

The memorial was dedicated on Memorial Day, 1962. And while it is called the USS Arizona Memorial, the memorial was dedicated to all who lost their lives on that Sunday morning, a date that still lives in infamy. United as never before, Americans mobilized and fought...and won. Then they helped the former enemy rebuild a broken nation. But the end of the war was not the beginning of peace. The next 50 years were a half-century of repression and brutality and new kinds of war.

For many Americans, history began on that violent Sunday at Pearl Harbor, and all future events were measured against the solemn import of that day.

The anchor of the USS Arizona, and its explanatory plaque, are part of the permanent memorial to all who died in the sudden Sunday raid.

The Pearl Harbor Naval Shipyard, as seen from the air. Inside the yard are specialty repair shops and four drydocks. The Japanese attack failed to destroy the Shipyard, allowing on-site repairs that might have been necessary 2,500 miles away on the U. S. West Coast had the Japanese attack destroyed or severely damaged the Shipyard.

HAWAII & PEARL HARBOR TODAY

When the attacking aircraft screamed over Pearl Harbor, pilots looked down on a harbor shaped like the palm of a hand, with fingers comprised of the four stretches of water–West, Middle, East, and Southeast Lochs. In the center was Ford Island, a mile and a quarter long and little more than half a mile wide. It was on the southeast side of Ford Island that seven battleships were moored on December 7, 1941.

Change came to Hawaii, no longer the somnolent military outpost it was in 1941. Still an important military bastion, the Islands achieved statehood (along with Alaska) in 1959 and entered a boom period that seemed to have no end. Investments from the U.S. Mainland in the wake of statehood spurred unprecedented development, not all of it desirable. The population soared from 422,770 in 1940 to 632,772 in 1960, then to 1,112,110 in 1989. The cost of living soared as well, as real estate became more scarce, hence more expensive. Honolulu attained the unenviable position of being the most expensive city in America when all cost factors were included. Tourism quickly outpaced all other industries, increasing from a few thousand visitors per year in 1941 to more than six million in 1990.

From the air today Pearl Harbor looks much the same – 12,000 acres of land and water containing more than 70 Navy commands, the working and/or housing place for over 20,000 sailors. There is a civilian working population of about 12,000, half of whom are employed in the 700-acre Pearl Harbor Naval Shipyard. The entire Pearl Harbor complex is valued at more than $6 billion. Its strategic value is incalculable.

The area got its name from the Hawaiians, who called it Wai Momi, the water of pearls, because of the oysters that lived in its waters. In 1840 U.S. Navy Lieutenant Charles Wilkes discovered that a dead reef blocked the harbor entrance, and believed that with its removal the harbor would be a significant shelter for ships. Other nations thought so too, and bidding for the site was spirited. In 1884, America won the bidding war when Hawaii received in exchange a reciprocity treaty that allowed Hawaiian sugar to enter the U.S. duty-free.

The war with Spain underscored the harbor's usefulness, and in 1900 dredging of the harbor entrance was started. In 1908 the Navy was directed to establish a naval station on the site. By 1916 Pearl Harbor ranked tenth in value among Navy bases, and the value kept growing right up to and beyond World War II. Peak employment at the important Naval Shipyard, however, came in World War II when 26,000 civilians worked on ships and submarines and kept America's Pacific Fleet in action.

Today some 40 ships are home-

A volcanic tuff cone and an ancient place of sacrifice, Punchbowl Crater now contains the National Memorial of the Pacific, where American dead from several wars rest.

ported at Pearl Harbor, and there is a large "mothball" fleet which could be recalled if needed. There are numerous piers and submarine pens, and a Naval Supply Center that is the largest store in the Pacific with its 180,000 items. An impressive building is the Commander, Naval Base, Headquarters. Near a stairwell in the headquarters is a plaque honoring the Combat Intelligence Unit of the 14th Naval District. In 1941 and 1942, under the direction of Lieutenant Commander Joseph J. Rochefort, the unit gleaned data from the Japanese codes that led to victories in the battles of Midway and the Coral Sea and the shooting down of Admiral Isoroku Yamamoto's aircraft.

Over the years Pearl Harbor has more than justified its role as first envisioned: as an outpost in the Pacific that is strategic, even vital, to U.S. operations.

Fifty years after the attack that scarred Oahu, Honolulu has grown to be a major metropolitan area.

CHAPTER 10

THE LESSON OF PEARL HARBOR

Official U.S. Navy Photograph

Fifty years after the attack on Pearl Harbor, the Navy officer in charge of all U.S. military forces in the Pacific was Admiral Charles R. Larson, who wore both pilot's wings and the golden dolphins of a submariner. He had a distinguished career prior to becoming Commander-in-Chief of the U.S. Pacific Fleet, and then Commander-in-Chief, Pacific. Throughout his career, Admiral Larson served in both operational and political posts, the classic training for a position in the Pacific where the commander is required to be diplomat as well as tactician.

A half-century after the attack, Admiral Larson replied to questions regarding Pearl Harbor:

Q: Does the rule still apply of no more than one aircraft carrier in Pearl Harbor at a given time?

A: No. Although it occurs infrequently, it is not uncommon to have two aircraft carriers in Pearl Harbor simultaneously.

Q: Who is in charge of air and sea defenses of Hawaii today, and are those defenses adequate to meet a conceivable threat?

A: Specifically, the Commander-in-Chief of the Pacific Fleet is in charge of the sea defense of Hawaii and the Commander-in-Chief of the Pacific Air Force is charged with the air defense of Hawaii. The defenses of Hawaii are more than adequate to meet any present or conceivable threat.

Q: Given the thawing of the Cold War, is it likely the Pacific Fleet will be reduced? Along these lines, do you perceive a lessening of the need to maintain a strong naval presence in Asia/Pacific?

A: The Pacific Fleet, like the Atlantic Fleet — and indeed the entire U.S. military — will be reduced in the coming years. There will still be a need, however, to maintain credible naval forces throughout the Pacific and Asian theaters. The smaller Pacific Fleet will be able to meet its commitments throughout the vast expanses of its area of responsibility.

Q: If sea power is an extension of U.S. diplomacy, how does this translate into specific missions for Pacific Fleet ships?

A: The presence of U.S. Navy ships throughout the Pacific is indeed a concrete show of U.S. interest in the region. Their presence, however, must be-and is-backed up by credible naval forces which have the ability to act in support of U.S. policy.

Q: Is it possible Pacific Fleet ships will be involved in anti-drug measures?

A: U.S. Pacific Fleet ships do, from time to time, participate in anti-drug operations.

Q: Do you foresee the closing of any major Naval installations in the Asia/Pacific region, including Hawaii?

A: With the smaller size of the Pacific Fleet in the future, there will of course be a corollary downsizing of the supporting facilities ashore as well. It is impossible to determine at this time, however, which facilities those will be or when they might be closed or reduced, and by what amount.

Q: Given today's radar and other devices, is it still possible an enemy task force could come within air-strike distance of Oahu's bases?

A: It is nearly impossible for any force, of any size, to approach Hawaii undetected today.

Q: What, in your view, are the lessons of Pearl Harbor — and are we in danger of forgetting them today?

A: The main lesson of Pearl Harbor is not to be caught unprepared. Since the close of the Second World War, the U.S. Navy has retained robust forces which it has operated all throughout the Pacific and Asian theater. Its level of preparedness is unprecedented in the history of our nation.

Q: Given the advance in weap-

With Kaneohe Bay and the Koolau Mountains as a backdrop, Marine Corps F/A-18 Hornet jets sit near the site of the seaplane ramps of 1941. Fifty years after the attack on Oahu, technology had made a single Hornet the match of numerous 1941 fighters.

onry, tactics, and technology, can you foresee a time when Pearl Harbor Naval Base will be outmoded and unnecessary as a base or for other use of Pacific Fleet ships?

A: The bases throughout Hawaii will be even more important in the future than they are today. That's because the geography of the vast Pacific will not change — it will still be as far from San Diego to Singapore or Bahrain tomorrow as it is today. Hawaii's geographic location makes it of extreme strategic value, especially in a time when the Fleet will not only be reduced, but during a time when our access to overseas bases may be reduced as well.

Symbol of sea power, the Trident submarine USS Nevada slips by the Arizona Memorial, not far from the place where her namesake was hit and then deliberately run aground to avoid blocking the harbor entrance.

On a sunny day in the National Memorial Cemetery of the Pacific, the Stars and Stripes send an unmistakable signal: that retribution is the aftermath of infamy, and that America is still the land of the free.

On a Sunday morning at Pearl Harbor the scene is calm and quiet. The breeze is a soft tradewind out of the northeast, and the little wavelets that lap against the ships and pilings are nudged by a gentle surge in the vast harbor. A visitor is reminded that ships come and go — men come and go — but elemental things remain: the wind and stars, the earth and the old, trackless ocean.

The churchbells ring and the visitor turns to go, one of millions who have paid their respects to the men who fought here. He strolls in the sunlight, one of the generation who will forever measure the events of their lives against the drama of that particular Sunday morning in Hawaii.

☆ ☆ ☆

ACKNOWLEDGEMENTS

The author assumes all responsibilities for any errors, but acknowledges significant assistance in the preparation of the text of this book. Although they are listed in the select bibliography, works by Gordon W. Prange and Hawaii's Dr. John J. Stephan must be singled out for their deep scholarship, their clarity and cohesiveness. Concepts from those books impacted strongly on my own research and my instinctive feelings about the Pearl Harbor attack and its aftermath. Also helpful were Richard Brady, Deputy Public Affairs Officer; Captain Jolene Keefer, USN; Commander Joel D. Keefer, USN; A.L. Wheeler and Petty Officer Ford of the Pearl Harbor Naval Base Public Affairs Office; Bill Dasher, Pearl Harbor SuBase Photo Lab and Joe DeMatto, SuBase Public Affairs Office; Capt. Taylor and Staff Sgt. Paro of Kaneohe Joint Public Affairs Office; Former Chief Ranger Jim Miculka of Guam's War in the Pacific National Historical Park; Bob Wernet, a Congressional aide who proved knowledgeable and interested in this project; Lieutenant Commander William P. (Dan) McDonnell, USN; Daniel Martinez, Park Historian for the USS Arizona Memorial National Park; Gary Beito, the Executive Director, Edean Saito, Business Manager, and Calvin Oshiro, Computer Specialist for the Arizona Memorial Museum Association; the Royal Hawaiian Hotel, for providing photographs; and my wife, Walelu, for her usual assistance and patience. A special gratitude must be expressed to Admiral Charles R. Larson, who at this writing was Commander in Chief of the Pacific Fleet and subsequently became Commander in Chief of all U.S. Pacific Forces. Admiral Larson set aside time during a particularly tense period involving a major national military effort to grant the interview recorded in part in these pages.

SELECT BIBLIOGRAPHY

Costello, John. *The Pacific War, 1941-1945*. New York: Quill, 1982.

Greene, Jack. *War at Sea, Pearl Harbor to Midway*. New York: Gallery Books, 1988.

Murphy, Thomas D. *Ambassadors in Arms*. Hawaii: University of Hawaii Press, 1955.

Prange, Gordon W. *At Dawn We Slept*. London and New York: Penguin Books edition, 1982.

Prange, Gordon W. *Pearl Harbor, The Verdict of History*. New York: McGraw-Hill, 1986.

Sheehan, Ed. *One Sunday Morning*. Hawaii: Island Heritage, 1971.

Slackman, Michael. *Historic Resource Study, USS Arizona Memorial*. Unpublished works in two volumes prepared for the National Park Service, United States Department of the Interior, 1984.

Stephan, John J. *Hawaii Under The Rising Sun*. Hawaii: University of Hawaii Press, 1984.

Stone, Scott C.S. *Pearl Harbor, The Way It Was*. Hawaii: Island Heritage, 1977.

Toland, John. *Infamy*. New York: Doubleday and Company, 1982.

Turnbull, S.R. *The Samurai*. New York: MacMillan, 1977.

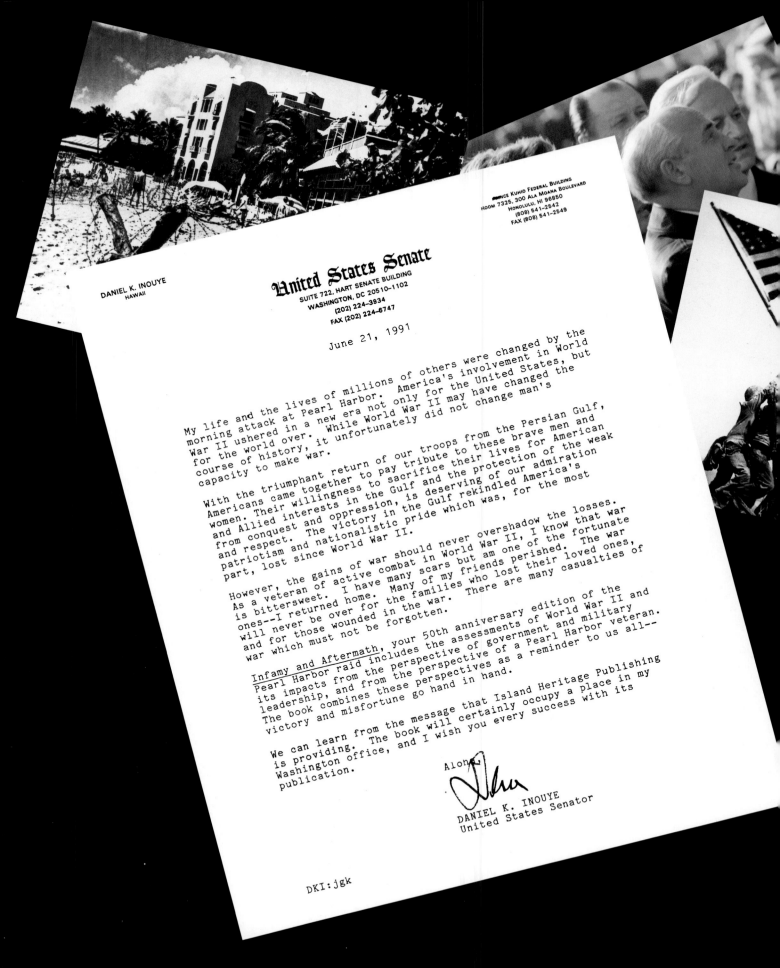

DANIEL K. INOUYE
HAWAII

United States Senate

SUITE 722, HART SENATE BUILDING
WASHINGTON, DC 20510–1102
(202) 224–3934
FAX (202) 224–6747

PRINCE KUHIO FEDERAL BUILDING
ROOM 7325, 300 ALA MOANA BOULEVARD
HONOLULU, HI 96850
(808) 541–2542
FAX (808) 541–2549

June 21, 1991

My life and the lives of millions of others were changed by the morning attack at Pearl Harbor. America's involvement in World War II ushered in a new era not only for the United States, but for the world over. While World War II may have changed the course of history, it unfortunately did not change man's capacity to make war.

With the triumphant return of our troops from the Persian Gulf, Americans came together to pay tribute to these brave men and women. Their willingness to sacrifice their lives for American and Allied interests in the Gulf and the protection of the weak from conquest and oppression, is deserving of our admiration and respect. The victory in the Gulf rekindled America's patriotism and nationalistic pride which was, for the most part, lost since World War II.

However, the gains of war should never overshadow the losses. As a veteran of active combat in World War II, I know that war is bittersweet. I have many scars but am one of the fortunate ones--I returned home. Many of my friends perished. The war will never be over for the families who lost their loved ones, and for those wounded in the war. There are many casualties of war which must not be forgotten.

<u>Infamy and Aftermath</u>, your 50th anniversary edition of the Pearl Harbor raid includes the assessments of World War II and its impacts from the perspective of government and military leadership, and from the perspective of a Pearl Harbor veteran. The book combines these perspectives as a reminder to us all-- victory and misfortune go hand in hand.

We can learn from the message that Island Heritage Publishing is providing. The book will certainly occupy a place in my Washington office, and I wish you every success with its publication.

Aloha,

DANIEL K. INOUYE
United States Senator

DKI:jgk

70

JOHN WAIHEE
GOVERNOR

EXECUTIVE CHAMBERS
HONOLULU

July 30, 1991

Today as we recall the tragic attack on Pearl Harbor fifty years ago, we reflect on history and its lessons for the future. Your publication, <u>Infamy & Aftermath, Pearl Harbor Then and Now</u>, is an important book in that it recalls the attack in detail and also examines the prelude to war and the postwar ramifications.

Hawaii, our nation and the world have all evolved and changed since 1941. Unfortunately, mankind's tendency to make war did not lessen after World War II, as evidenced by conflicts around the globe. <u>Infamy & Aftermath</u> brings into focus the geopolitical events of our era. Through this special recollection of war, we underscore the human face on war. It also recounts personal vignettes which put a significance of our quest for peace and the consequences of our failure to achieve it.

<u>Infamy & Aftermath</u> has both a serious theme and a lively style. I am pleased to see a work of this significance written and produced by island people about an event which means so much to all of us.

With kindest regards,

Sincerely,

John Waihee

JOHN WAIHEE

SCOTT C. S. STONE is a novelist and historian, and the author of numerous other books for which he holds top writing awards including an "Edgar" for suspense fiction. He is a veteran Asia/Pacific correspondent who writes for international media. Stone is also a former Navy Commander (Reserve) with extended periods of active duty including clandestine paramilitary operations in various parts of Asia. He now lives with his wife, Walelu, on the Island of Hawaii.